INSTANT GAMES FOR CHiLDREN'S MiNiSTRY

BY SUSAN L. LiNGO

Group

Loveland, Colorado

DEDICATION

TO MY MOM, PEGGY, AND
HER LOVING, PLAYFUL HEART:
THANKS FOR TEACHING ME
THERE'S JOY WHEN WE'RE AT
PLAY IN OUR LORD!

INSTANT GAMES FOR CHILDREN'S MINISTRY

Copyright © 1995 Susan L. Lingo

Credits
Book Acquisitions Editor: Mike Nappa
Editor: Jody Brolsma
Senior Editor/Creative Products Director: Joani Schultz
Copy Editor: Janis Sampson
Cover Art Director: Liz Howe
Designer: Lisa Smith
Computer Graphic Artist: Anne Vetter
Cover Photographer: Craig DeMartino
Illustrator: Rebecca Thornburgh
Production Manager: Gingar Kunkel

Unless otherwise noted, Scriptures quoted from The Youth Bible, New Century Version, copyright © 1991 by Word Publishing, Dallas, Texas 75039. Used by permission.

Library of Congress Cataloging-in-Publication Data
Lingo, Susan L.
    Instant games for children's ministry / by Susan L. Lingo.
       p. cm.
    Includes indexes.
    ISBN 1-55945-695-7
    1. Games in Christian education. I. Title.
  BV1536.3.L56   1995
  268'.432—dc20
                                   95-18765
                                       CIP

Printed in the United States of America.
10 9 8 7 6 5 4 3 2   04 03 02 01 00 99 98 97 96

CONTENTS

THE GAMES!

INTRODUCTION

THE KEY TO GAME CONFIDENCE

Kids love to play games. But coming up with new and exciting games to play with your kids is often frustrating and collecting game equipment can be costly and time consuming. Not anymore! *Instant Games for Children's Ministry* is a collection of fast-paced, fun-to-play games for every child in your class. And all playing pieces are at your fingertips any time, anyplace.

The key to successfully playing games with children may be summed up in two words: *game confidence!* When you're familiar with a myriad of exciting games and have the equipment to play them, games can be an enriching time of fellowship for everyone.

WHY PLAY GAMES?

No children's ministry program can be built on games alone—yet the effective use of game-time helps nurture many positive benefits, including

- community building,
- getting acquainted,
- burning excess energy to help kids refocus,
- strengthening teamwork and cooperation, and
- creating a welcoming, positive atmosphere.

Games that foster *cooperation*, instead of competition, help kids feel accepted and successful with peers and leaders. The games included in *Instant Games for Children's Ministry* are cooperative and not based on "winners" and "losers"—everyone is a winner in the good-time department!

HOW INSTANT GAMES WORK

Each game in *Instant Games for Children's Ministry* uses an item from the handy game tote that is quickly assembled by "shopping" your home, discount stores, garage sales, other church members, or close-out stores. Here are the simple items you'll need to play 101 different games.

roll of masking tape   2 Ping-Pong balls

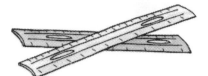

2 rulers

playground ball

foam ball

6 plastic tumblers or cups

6 circular foam coasters or disks

2 jump-ropes

bag of balloons

2 bandannas

kitchen timer

color cube and number cube (explained below)

Assemble these simple, inexpensive items in a pillowcase, laundry basket, box, or trash bag, and you'll be ready any time you or your kids say, "Let's play a game!"

To make the color and number cubes, simply cover two small square boxes with white self-adhesive shelf paper. For the color cube, use permanent markers to color the sides red, yellow, green, and blue. You'll use two colors twice. For the number cube, use a marker to add numerals and dots to represent numbers from one through four. Again, you'll use two numbers twice.

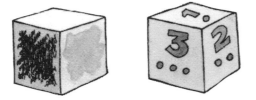

HAVE A BLAST!

That's all there is to it! You're now ready to energize your kids by offering them a wonderful selection of games that are sure to become group favorites. And best of all, these games will travel with your group inside, outside, to the gymnasium, on picnics, and to retreats.

So go wild. Be daring. And have a blast playing games with your kids as you all share in the joy of fellowship and fun!

TAXi! TAXi!

GET SET...

OBJECT OF THE GAME: Find a matching taxicab and be the first pair to snatch the *cup*.

GO!

DIRECTIONS: Set the *cup* at one end of the playing area and gather kids at the opposite end. Form two groups and designate one group as the Taxicabs and the other as the Riders. Have groups stand a few feet apart. Direct the Taxis to secretly number off by fours.

Say: **It's a rainy day, and there aren't many taxis for people to ride in! I'll roll the *number cube* and call out, "Taxi #2," or whatever number is rolled. Riders, race to find a Taxi that matches that number by asking Taxis their numbers. Then Taxi and Rider can lock arms and rush to pick up the *cup*.**

After each round, have the Taxicabs secretly renumber themselves. When you've played a few rounds, switch roles so the Riders become the Taxicabs.

> ## INSIDE TIP
>
> For an exciting twist, have each Rider choose a color from the *color cube*. Then roll both the *number* and *color cubes* to find matching Riders and Taxis.

WALK THE LINE

GET SET...

OBJECT OF THE GAME: As your partner deflects the ball, safely deliver a *bandanna* from one end of the line to the other.

GO!

DIRECTIONS: Form two lines and stand facing each other three feet apart. Lay *bandannas* at the ends of each line (see diagram). Hand the *playground ball* to a child in the middle of one line. Designate one line the Guards and one line the Grabbers. The kids opposite each other at the ends of the lines are partners.

Say: **When I say "go," the partners from the ends of each line will go to the *bandannas*. The Grabbers will each pick up a *bandanna* and walk between the lines while you try to tag them with the ball. Guards can block the shots to keep their partners safe. If the Grabber makes it to the opposite end of the line without being tagged, he or she sets the *bandanna* down and both partners go to the middle of the lines to wait their next turn. If a Grabber is tagged, the Grabber and Guard aren't eligible to walk the line again, but they can return to the line to help tag others. Then the next partners on the ends walk the line.**

Have pairs take turns walking the line until there's only one pair that hasn't been tagged.

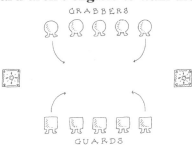

PANIC PASS

GET READY...

GROUP SIZE: Any
BEST FOR GRADES: 1-6
PLAYING TIME: 15 minutes
ENERGY LEVEL: Medium
ITEMS NEEDED: All game items

GET SET...

OBJECT OF THE GAME: Don't get caught without an item when the passing frenzy stops!

GO!

DIRECTIONS: Sit in a circle on the floor. Choose one child to be the Roller and give him or her the *color cube*. Instruct the Roller to sit in the center of the circle. Let each player choose one game item to hold.

> **INSIDE TIP**
> Help kids remember the color code by comparing it to a stoplight. Red is stop, yellow is slow down, and green is go or speed up!

Say: **This is a speedy passing game! We'll start passing the items around the circle to the right. Be sure you're holding only one item at a time. The Roller will roll the *color cube* and call out the color rolled. If the color is blue, we'll reverse the passing direction; if the color is yellow, we'll slow down; if the color is green, we'll speed up the passing; and if the color is red, we'll stop. If we stop, and you're caught without an item or with more than one item, come to the center and help the Roller. We'll remove an item for each person who comes to the center. Let's play until there are only two players left in the circle.**

Begin passing items to the right. Be sure to remove an item each time someone goes to the center of the circle. (There should always be one item for each person in the circle.)

TiGHTROPE TOSS

GET READY...

GROUP SIZE: 6 or more
BEST FOR GRADES: K-6
PLAYING TIME: 10 minutes
ENERGY LEVEL: Medium
ITEMS NEEDED: The *foam ball*, the *playground ball*, and the *masking tape*

GET SET...

OBJECT OF THE GAME: Walk the "tightrope" while tossing and catching balls.

GO!

DIRECTIONS: Create a 5-foot square "tightrope" on the floor using *masking tape*. If you have six to eight kids, make a triangular tightrope. Direct kids to line up around the tightrope. (Be sure there are kids on each side of the tightrope.) Hand two children the balls.

Say: **In this death-defying circus act, you must walk the wobbly tightrope as you toss the balls to each other! If you drop a ball or step off the tightrope, come sit in the center. Center people may call out directions such as "hop," "change directions," or "walk backward." Tightrope walkers must follow those directions. We'll play until there are only two tightrope walkers left.**

> **INSIDE TIP**
>
> Older kids may enjoy walking the tightrope in pairs. Have partners hook arms and walk sideways around the tightrope.

THE PITS

GET READY...

GROUP SIZE: 8 or more
BEST FOR GRADES: 2-6
PLAYING TIME: 15 minutes
ENERGY LEVEL: High
ITEMS NEEDED: The *masking tape*, 2 *jump-ropes*, 6 *cups*, and the *playground ball*

GET SET...

OBJECT OF THE GAME: Work as a group to knock over your opponents' *cups*.

Go!

DIRECTIONS: This game is best suited for a gymnasium or outside play. Divide the playing area in half with a 5-foot line of *masking tape*. Lay each *jump-rope* 20 feet away from the center line to create "Pit Zones." Set three *cups* at random on each side of the center line (see diagram). Form two groups and have them stand on opposite sides of the center line.

INSIDE TIP

Older children may enjoy using the *foam ball* and the *playground ball* simultaneously. For another twist, have kids use their feet instead of their hands to roll the ball.

Say: **This game may be called the Pits, but you'll have a great time playing! The object is to knock over the other group's *cups*. You may roll the *playground ball* with your hands to knock *cups* over, and you may also block shots from hitting your *cups*. But each time a *cup* on your side is toppled, one of your players must go to the Pit Zone on the other side. He or she stays there until someone in your group rolls the ball to him or her. Then that player may safely return to your side and set up a *cup*. We'll play until one side has all the *cups* knocked over.**

SPLASH-DOWN!

✷ GET READY...

GROUP SIZE: 4 or more
BEST FOR GRADES: K-6
PLAYING TIME: 15 minutes per round
ENERGY LEVEL: High
ITEMS NEEDED: 2 *cups*, 2 *Ping-Pong balls*, 2 *bandannas*, and water

✷ GET SET...

OBJECT OF THE GAME: Be the astronauts with the most water in your "splashdown" *cup* at the end of the game.

✷ GO!

DIRECTIONS: This game is best played outside in the summer. Be sure kids are wearing clothes that can get damp from some splashy fun!

Fill two *cups* with water. Form two groups of "astronauts" and hand each group a *Ping-Pong ball* and a *bandanna*. Direct each group to choose an astronaut to go first. Hand him or her a splashdown *cup*. Set a *Ping-Pong ball* in the center of each *bandanna* and instruct group members to hold a portion of this "launch pad."

Say: **Every astronaut wants a great splashdown. We'll pretend the *Ping-Pong balls* are rocket ships and launch them into orbit. Then the astronauts with the *cups* will race to make great splashdowns and catch the rocket ships. If you catch your rocket ship, trade places with another astronaut in your group. If you miss, try again.** Encourage kids to shout group countdowns by saying, "Three, two, one, blastoff!" as they launch the *Ping-Pong balls* in the air using the *bandannas*.

Continue launching and catching the rocket ships until all the astronauts have made successful splashdowns. Let the group with the most water left in the *cup* line up first for refreshments.

> **iNSiDE TiP**
>
> For an indoor variation, have kids launch the *disks* or the *number* and *color cubes* and then catch them with their hands, instead of with the *cups*.

ACTiON SUBTRAC-TiON

GET SET...

GET READY...

GROUP SIZE: 10 or more
BEST FOR GRADES: 2-6
PLAYING TIME: 10 minutes
ENERGY LEVEL: Low
ITEM NEEDED: The *number cube*

OBJECT OF THE GAME: Use group strategy to subtract the "numbers" in a number line.

Go!

DIRECTIONS: Choose eight kids to stand in front of the group. (You may choose 10 kids if your group is very large.) Help them number off one through eight (or 10). Direct the children to hold up their assigned number using their fingers. These are the "Number Kids." Have the other children find partners.

Say: **Let's play a game called Action Subtraction. We'll try to subtract Number Kids until there's no one left standing in the number line. Partners will roll the *number cube*, then decide which Number Kids to subtract. For example, if a two and four are**

> **iNSiDE TiP**
>
> Older kids may enjoy a special challenge! Have pairs play against each other and either *add* or *subtract* Number Kids to prevent the other side from going out. Game ends when one side finally subtracts all the Number Kids.

rolled, number six may sit down because two plus four equals six, or numbers two and four may sit down. If there's no one to sit down with the numbers rolled, pass the *number cube* to the next pair.

Play until all of the Number Kids are sitting down. Then choose new Number Kids to take their places. Continue until everyone has been a Number Kid at least once.

TWO ARE BETTER THAN ONE

GET READY...

GROUP SIZE: Any
BEST FOR GRADES: K-3
PLAYING TIME: 15 minutes
ENERGY LEVEL: Medium
ITEMS NEEDED: 2 *jump-ropes*, a *cup*, and 2 *bandannas*

GET SET...

OBJECT OF THE GAME: Travel with your partner in a wacky way and be the first pair to snatch the *cup*.

GO!

DIRECTIONS: Lay the *jump-ropes* end to end as a starting line. Place the *cup* 20 feet away from the starting line. Form two groups and have children find partners within their groups. (If there's an extra child, form a trio.)

Say: **Some things are easier to do when you have friends to help. You can help your partners in this game. Huddle with your partner and decide how you'll travel from the starting line to the *cup*. You can travel in wacky ways such as rolling over and over or hopping or standing on your partner's feet and walking. Oh, there's just one rule: You must have your legs fastened to your partner's legs with a *bandanna!***

When kids have had a moment to decide on their mode of travel, have the first two pairs step to the starting line. Loosely tie their legs together with the *bandannas*. Invite everyone to say, "Ready, set, go!" Have the first pair to reach the *cup* hold it in the air. Continue until each pair has had a turn. Then encourage each player to give his or her partner a pat on the back for the help.

TRIANGLE TANGLE BALL

★ GET READY...

GROUP SIZE: 8 or more
BEST FOR GRADES: 1-6
PLAYING TIME: 15 minutes
ENERGY LEVEL: High
ITEMS NEEDED: The *jump-rope*, 6 *cups*, 2 *bandannas*, a *disk*, and the *playground ball*

★ GET SET...

OBJECT OF THE GAME: Travel safely around the triangle and score *"cups"* for your group.

★ GO!

DIRECTIONS: This game is best suited for outdoor play and is similar to kickball. Lay the *jump-rope* on the ground for home base. Set six *cups* beside home base. Place the *bandannas* 20 feet from the *jump-rope* at outward angles (see diagram). The *jump-rope* and *bandannas* should form the points of a triangle with 20 feet between each point. Place the *disk* in the center of the triangle.

Have kids get into two groups: the Fielders and the Kickers. Tell the Fielders to choose a Roller and have the Roller stand on the *disk* while holding the *playground ball*. The other Fielders will guard the *bandannas*.

Say: **This is a game played like the ol' American favorite—baseball! In this game, when the Roller rolls you the ball, you'll kick the ball and try to run the bases without getting tagged. On the way to home base, pick up a *cup* to score 1 point for your group. We'll switch Fielders and Kickers after three people are tagged out.**

Continue playing until there are three outs, then Fielders and Kickers switch places. The game is over when all the *cups* have been grabbed.

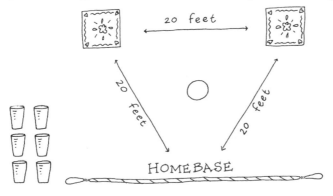

HOME BASE

HELPING HANDBALL

GET READY...

GROUP SIZE: 8 or more
BEST FOR GRADES: 1-6
PLAYING TIME: 10 minutes
ENERGY LEVEL: High
ITEMS NEEDED: The *masking tape* and the *playground ball*

GET SET...

OBJECT OF THE GAME: Help your partner dodge the ball and be the last pair in the game.

Go!

DIRECTIONS: Run a 10-foot strip of *masking tape* down the center of the playing area. Form two groups and have each group stand on opposite sides of the center line. Direct kids to find partners within their groups.

> **INSIDE TIP**
>
> Remind kids to throw the ball at or below waist level. You may want to impose a penalty for shots above the waist, such as a two-minute timeout for the tosser.

Say: **This is an exciting game, but you'll need to rely on your partner's help! We'll play the game like Dodge Ball, but if the ball tags your arm or leg, you can't use that arm or leg for the rest of the game. For example, if one arm is hit with the ball, you must put that arm behind your back and use only the other arm. Or if both arms are hit, you may use only your feet and legs and your partner will throw the ball for you. If your leg is hit, you'll have to lean on your partner for support. And if both your legs are hit, you'll have to sit down, and your partner will toss the ball and guard you. If you're hit while sitting down, you're out.**

Bounce the *playground ball* into the playing area to begin the game. Continue playing until there's only one set of partners remaining.

SiLLY SCARF

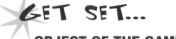

GET READY...

GROUP SIZE: Any
BEST FOR GRADES: K-6
PLAYING TIME: 15 minutes
ENERGY LEVEL: Low
ITEMS NEEDED: 2 *jump-ropes*, a *bandanna*, and the *color cube*

GET SET...

OBJECT OF THE GAME: Be the first to snatch the *color cube* in this game of giggles and grins.

Go!

DIRECTIONS: Place the *jump-ropes* at one end of the playing area as the starting line. Choose one child to hold the *bandanna* and stand at least 15 feet from the starting line. Set the *color cube* beside the child holding the *bandanna*. Instruct the other kids to stand on the starting line.

Say: **Laughing makes us feel great—but once you start laughing, can you stop? When the** *bandanna* **is dropped, start laughing. Then walk toward the** *color cube*. **But watch out because when the** *bandanna* **is picked up, you must stop laughing and freeze in place. No giggles—no grins! If you laugh before the** *bandanna* **is dropped, you must return to the starting line and begin again. The first one to pick up the** *color cube* **is the next** *bandanna* **dropper.**

Play until you've had two or three *bandanna* droppers. You may wish to add a different twist by having kids hop or crawl to the *color cube*, instead of walk.

BELLY BOPPiN'

GET READY...

GROUP SIZE: Any
BEST FOR GRADES: 2-6
PLAYING TIME: 10 minutes
ENERGY LEVEL: Medium
ITEMS NEEDED: The *balloons*

GET SET...

OBJECT OF THE GAME: Be the first pair to bop 'n' pop your *balloons*.

Go!

DIRECTIONS: Blow up and tie off a *balloon* for each child in your group. Have kids find partners. If there's an uneven number of children in your class, a trio will work. Distribute a *balloon* to each pair.

INSIDE TIP

This is a great ice-breaker for kickoff parties at the beginning of the year. Provide a few more *balloons* and let kids switch partners to pop *balloons* by sitting on them or stomping on them.

Say: **What's more fun than balloons and friends? We'll use both to play this exciting game! When I say "bop-bop-bop," tap your *balloon* back and forth in the air. When I say "Pop!" grab your *balloon* and wedge it between your partner's tummy and your own. Bop against the *balloons* until they pop. When your *balloon* pops, shout, "Bopped 'n' popped!"**

After all the *balloons* are popped, have kids find new partners. Then repeat the game having kids wedge their *balloons* against their backs or knees to pop them.

FOX AND HOUNDS

GET READY...

GROUP SIZE: Any
BEST FOR GRADES: K-3
PLAYING TIME: 10 minutes
ENERGY LEVEL: High
ITEMS NEEDED: 2 *bandannas*

GET SET...

OBJECT OF THE GAME: Grab the Fox's tail before he gets to his den.

Go!

DIRECTIONS: Have kids sit or stand in a circle. Choose one child to be the Fox and hand him or her the *bandannas*. Direct the Fox to tuck one of the *bandannas* inside his or her waistband or belt so it hangs down like a tail. (If the child has no waistband or belt, have the child simply hold the *bandanna* in back at the waist like a tail.)

Say: **This is a speedy, sly Fox. The rest of you are Hounds who like to chase foxes. The Fox will walk around the circle holding a *bandanna*. If the Fox drops the *bandanna* behind you, pick it up and chase the Fox. If you snatch the Fox's tail before he or she gets around the circle to your place, you're faster than a fox! But if the Fox gets safely to your place, you become the next Fox.**

Play until everyone has had a chance to chase the Fox. Instead of running each time, have children crawl, hop, walk backward, or walk heel to toe around the circle.

CLOSET CLEAN-OUT

GET READY...

GROUP SIZE: 8 or more
BEST FOR GRADES: 1-4
PLAYING TIME: 15 minutes
ENERGY LEVEL: Medium
ITEMS NEEDED: The *masking tape*, 6 *cups*, 6 *disks*, a *bandanna*, 2 *Ping-Pong balls*, the *number cube*, and the *kitchen timer*

GET SET...

OBJECT OF THE GAME: Be the group with the cleanest "closet" when time runs out.

Go!

DIRECTIONS: Divide your playing area in half using a *masking tape* line. Form two groups and have groups stand on opposite sides of the line. Place three *cups*, three *disks*, a *bandanna*, and a *Ping-Pong ball* on each side of the center line. Set the *number cube* on the line.

Say: **Cleaning out closets is a lot of work, but in**

INSIDE TIP

Add extra excitement and "cleaning frenzy" by challenging groups *not* to get caught with the *number cube* on their side when time runs out.

this game it's a lot of fun, too! When I begin the timer and say "go," race to toss things out of your closet and over the center line into *your* neighbor's closet. But watch out because they'll be tossing stuff back into *your* closet just as quickly! Keep cleaning those closets until time runs out. Then we'll see who has the cleanest closet in the neighborhood!

Begin the timer and say "go." After one round of play, form two new groups and play again. When the games are over, encourage kids to give each other handshakes and say, "You're a great cleanin' machine!"

HUMAN TUG O' WAR

GET READY...

GROUP SIZE: 8 or more
BEST FOR GRADES: 4-6
PLAYING TIME: 10 minutes
ENERGY LEVEL: Medium
ITEMS NEEDED: The *masking tape* and 4 *cups*

GET SET...

OBJECT OF THE GAME: Do the "strongman stretch" and be the first to snatch a *cup*.

GO!

DIRECTIONS: Use the *masking tape* to mark off a 7-foot square on the floor, then set a *cup* at each corner. Place a small *masking tape* X in the center of the square. Have kids find partners.

Say: **Put on your strongman muscles—we're going to stretch and reach in this game.** Choose two pairs. Have each partner A place a foot on the X and join hands. Have each partner B loop one arm around partner A's waist (see diagram).

Say: **When I say "go," tug on each other and be the first pair to snatch a *cup* from one of the corners. Don't let go of your partner's waist or the other pair automatically wins the round.**

Continue until each pair has had a turn to pull. For older kids, try using four pairs and have a four-way Tug o' War (see diagram).

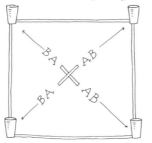

MiNEFiELD

GET READY...

GROUP SIZE: Any
BEST FOR GRADES: K-2
PLAYING TIME: 10 minutes
ENERGY LEVEL: Medium
ITEMS NEEDED: A *jump-rope*, 2 *bandannas*, 6 *disks*, 6 *cups*, the *foam ball*, and 2 *Ping-Pong balls*

GET SET...

OBJECT OF THE GAME: Work your way safely through the course without touching any obstacles.

GO!

DIRECTIONS: Establish start and finish lines using a *jump-rope* and the *bandannas*. Invite kids to scatter the *disks*, *cups*, *foam ball*, and *Ping-Pong balls* between the lines as make-believe explosive mines. When the obstacles are all "planted," have kids find partners and decide who'll be the Guide and who'll be the Creeper.

> **INSIDE TIP**
> This game is great reinforcement for the concepts of cooperation, communication, and reliance.

Say: **There are pretend mines planted all over the course. Creepers, your mission is to make it safely through the minefield by listening carefully to the directions your Guide gives you. There's one rule: Creepers must keep their eyes closed at all times! When you cross the finish line, Creepers and Guides will switch places and return to the**

starting line. If you bump into a mine, you and your partner must freeze in place and count to 10 out loud before
continuing.

If you have younger kids in your group, let the Creepers walk
through the minefield and hold the hands of their Guides.

WiGGLe WORM

★ GET READY...

GROUP SIZE: Any
BEST FOR GRADES: K-2
PLAYING TIME: 10 minutes
ENERGY LEVEL: Medium
ITEMS NEEDED: 2 *jump-ropes*
and 2 *bandannas*

★ GET SET...

OBJECT OF THE GAME: Make a cooperative, wiggling
"worm" that reaches to the finish line.

★ Go!

DIRECTIONS: Lay the *jump-ropes* at one end of the playing
area as the starting line. Place the *bandannas* at the opposite end
as the finish line. Have kids form two or three groups and line up
behind the starting line.

> ★ **iNSiDE TiP**
>
> For a fun twist,
> scatter a few ob-
> stacles along the
> way, then have the
> entire class create
> one wiggly worm
> to travel around
> the obstacles from
> start to finish.

Say: **If you've ever watched wiggly
worms crawl, you know they really
s-t-r-e-t-c-h out! We're going to stretch
our way to the finish line. When I say
"Wiggle!" the first person in each
worm-line can get on their tummy and
stretch his or her arms out in front.
Then the next person lays in front with
his or her feet in the hands of the first
player and so on. When everyone is
lying down, the person at the back of the worm-line jumps
up and runs to the front. Continue until your worm reaches the finish line.**

MAKE A WISH

GET READY...

GROUP SIZE: Up to 20
BEST FOR GRADES: K-6
PLAYING TIME: 15 minutes
ENERGY LEVEL: Low
ITEMS NEEDED: The *number cube* and a game item for each child

GET SET...

OBJECT OF THE GAME: Exercise your amazing memory skills and collect different items from other players.

Go!

DIRECTIONS: Sit in a circle on the floor and have kids number off by fours. Place a grab bag item for each child in the center and allow each one to choose an item to hold. Direct children to hold their items up for 15 seconds and encourage kids to remember who has which item. After 15 seconds, have kids hide the items in their laps.

Roll the *number cube* and call out the number rolled. Each player with that number gets to ask for an item by pointing at another player and saying, "I wish for a (name of the item that child is holding)." If the appointed player has the item wished for, he or she must give it to the "wisher." Continue until everyone has "wished" for an item at least two times. At the end of the game, the players with the most items get to line up first for treats or drinks.

PARTNER PULLEY-TAG

GET READY...

GROUP SIZE: 6 or more
BEST FOR GRADES: K-6
PLAYING TIME: 15 minutes
ENERGY LEVEL: High
ITEM NEEDED: The *playground ball*

GET SET...

OBJECT OF THE GAME: Tag opposing partners until only one pair is standing.

GO!

DIRECTIONS: Form pairs and decide who's the Scooper and who's the Tosser. Have pairs lock arms.

Say: **We all enjoy a good game of Tag. But this game of Tag has a new twist: You'll work with partners to tag others. Each partner has an important job—Scoopers can only pick up the ball, and Tossers can only throw it. You'll have to work cooperatively to tag others, and you must stay locked to your partner's arms. If either partner gets tagged by the ball, you both must sit down. We'll play until there's only one pair left standing. If you're tagged out, cheer the others on.**

Toss the *playground ball* into the playing area to begin the game. Continue playing until one pair is standing. Play the game a second time having Scoopers and Tossers switch roles.

HOCUS-POCUS HATS

GET READY...

GROUP SIZE: 8 or more
BEST FOR GRADES: K-2
PLAYING TIME: 10 minutes
ENERGY LEVEL: Low
ITEMS NEEDED: 6 *cups* and 2 *Ping-Pong balls*

GET SET...

OBJECT OF THE GAME: Hide and then seek the *Ping-Pong ball* in this simple guessing game.

GO!

DIRECTIONS: Form two groups: the Ali group and the Kazam group. Hand each group three *cups* and a *Ping-Pong ball*. Tell groups to choose three people to wear the *cups* like hats. Then invite the groups to form huddles and secretly slide their *Ping-Pong ball* under one of their "hats." Tell kids to hold the hats on their heads.

Say: **We'll take turns guessing where the *Ping-Pong balls* are hidden. One person from each group can remove one of their opponent's hats. If the *Ping-Pong ball* is under that**

hat, you may choose someone from that group to join your group. If the *Ping-Pong ball* isn't under that hat, you must join the other group. After five rounds we'll see which group has the most members.

Before you finish playing, be sure everyone has had a chance to wear a hat at least once.

INSIDE TIP

This is a great game to use with young children for *icebreakers* and beginning-of-the-year parties.

SUPER RACERS

GET READY...

GROUP SIZE: Any
BEST FOR GRADES: K-4
PLAYING TIME: 15 minutes
ENERGY LEVEL: Medium
ITEMS NEEDED: A *balloon*, a *disk*, a *cup*, a *bandanna*, a *Ping-Pong ball*, and the *color cube*

GET SET...

OBJECT OF THE GAME: Be the first to pass your racer around the racetrack.

GO!

DIRECTIONS: Blow up and tie off the *balloon*. Have kids sit in a circle and place the *balloon*, the *disk*, the *cup*, the *bandanna*, the *Ping-Pong ball*, and the *color cube* in the center. Choose two children to be Senders and have them each pick an item to use as a "racer."

INSIDE TIP

For extra fun have three or four racers speeding in different directions simultaneously!

Say: **It's a fine day at the races, and you've chosen some unusual racers. We're going to speed-pass the racers around the circle, but first the Senders will tell us how to pass their racers. For example, "The (item) will be passed under your knees" or "The (item) will be passed behind your back." When I say "go," Senders can pass their racers in opposite directions. The racer that makes it back to the Sender first will race against someone else in the next round.**

Begin the game and have children pass the racers in opposite directions. Be sure kids are passing the racers in the specified manners. At the end of the first race, have the child whose racer finished second return his or her item to the center of the circle and choose someone else to race. Continue until everyone has had a turn to race an item.

BALANCiNG ACT

GET READY...

GROUP SIZE: 4 or more
BEST FOR GRADES: K-2
PLAYING TIME: 10 minutes
ENERGY LEVEL: Medium
ITEMS NEEDED: 2 *bandannas*, 6 *disks*, 6 *cups*, 2 *rulers*, and the *color* and *number cubes*

GET SET...

OBJECT OF THE GAME: Work with your partner to balance items on head or shoulders and then walk to the finish line together.

GO!

DIRECTIONS: Establish start and finish lines by placing *bandannas* at opposite ends of the playing area. Place the *disks*, the cups, and the *rulers* behind the finish line. Have kids get into red, yellow, blue, and green color groups and find partners in their groups. Have them choose which partner will be the first Balancer, then have partners stand behind the starting line.

Say: **This game is a real balancing act! I'll roll the *color* and *number cubes*. Let's say we roll a three and the color red. The red partners will hop to the finish line. The Balancer in each pair will balance three items on his or her head and shoulders. Then the pair will return to the starting line. If any items drop, the partner without the items must pick up** the fallen objects and replace them on the Balancer's head

> **INSIDE TIP**
>
> If you have a small group, this game may be played without partners. Vary the places items may be balanced. For example, create a balancing act with your elbows and the backs of your hands, or with your knees and your nose.

or shoulders. When you reach the starting line, switch roles and return to the finish line.

FiELD FOOTBALL

GET READY...

GROUP SIZE: 6 or more
BEST FOR GRADES: 2-6
PLAYING TIME: 15 minutes or longer
ENERGY LEVEL: High
ITEMS NEEDED: The *playground ball*, 2 *jump-ropes*, 2 *bandannas*, and 6 *cups*

GET SET...

OBJECT OF THE GAME: Using only your feet, try to knock over your opponents' *cups*.

Go!

DIRECTIONS: Establish goal lines by placing the *jump-ropes* 50 feet apart. Set three *cups* one foot apart in front of each *jump-rope*. Lay the *bandannas* in the center of the playing area. Form team A and team B and direct them to stand on opposite sides of the *bandannas*.

Say: **This game is called football because we'll only use our feet to play. I'll roll the *playground ball* down the center of the playing area. Use your feet to roll and kick the ball to knock over the *cups* on your opponents' side. If you use your hands, you must join the other group. Stay on your own side of the center area! We'll play until one side has all their *cups* knocked down.**

For older groups, dispense with the *bandannas* and let players move over the entire field.

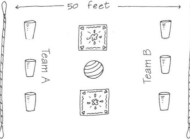

CRAZY CONCEN- TRATiON

GET READY...

GROUP SIZE: 8 or more
BEST FOR GRADES: K-2
PLAYING TIME: 10 minutes
ENERGY LEVEL: Low
ITEMS NEEDED: Pairs of items such as 2 *Ping-Pong balls*, 3 pairs of *cups*, 2 *rulers*, 2 *bandannas*, 2 *balloons*, or 2 *jump-ropes*

GET SET...

OBJECT OF THE GAME: Give your memory a workout by matching pairs of items.

Go!

DIRECTIONS: Invite each child to choose a game item from those you've set out. Then direct kids to sit in a circle and hide their items in their laps.

iNSiDE TiP

For a great memory-match warm-up, line up five or six items and let kids look at them for a few seconds. Then hide the items and have kids recall what objects were shown and their order in line.

Say: **Let's exercise our memories. We'll take turns finding pairs of items and placing them in the center when a match is made.** Choose a child to show his or her object and then point to the player believed to hold the matching object. If the guess is correct, have the child place the pair of items in the center. If guess is incorrect, both players again hide their items and someone else has a turn. The children whose items are matched may still point to players to find matching pairs. Continue playing until all the matching items are in the center. Have children play once more but let them choose new items to match.

FAST-FooD FRENZY

GET READY...

GROUP SIZE: 6 or more
BEST FOR GRADES: K-6
PLAYING TIME: 10 minutes
ENERGY LEVEL: High
ITEMS NEEDED: 2 *rulers* and 2 *jump-ropes*

GET SET...

OBJECT OF THE GAME: Be fast food and get bagged—not tagged!

GO!

DIRECTIONS: Establish a starting line by laying both *rulers* at one end of the playing area. Make two *jump-rope* circles about 20 feet from the starting line. Tell kids the circles are the fast-food "bags." Let children decide which of the following fast-food items they'll be:

- hamburgers,
- tacos, or
- french fries,
- shakes.

Choose one person to be the Caller. Then instruct all the fast food to stand behind the starting line.

INSIDE TIP

Let older kids really whoop it up by allowing them to call as many fast-food items as they want, using only one bag! You may want to vary the mode of travel to hopping, walking backward, or crawling to the bags. Be sure the Caller moves in the same way as the "food."

Say: **This is a game of really fast food! The Caller will name one or two fast-food items. The players who chose those food items will run to stand in the bags (*jump-rope* circles) before the Caller tags them. In other words, you want to get bagged before you're tagged! Anyone who's tagged helps the Caller tag more fast-food items.**

Continue playing until all the food items have been tagged. The last player tagged becomes the next Caller.

MONKEY MAZE

GET READY...

GROUP SIZE: 8 or more
BEST FOR GRADES: K-2
PLAYING TIME: 15 minutes
ENERGY LEVEL: Medium
ITEMS NEEDED: The *kitchen timer* and 1 game item for each player

GET SET...

OBJECT OF THE GAME: Work your way through a crazy maze of Monkeys before time runs out.

GO!

DIRECTIONS: Set out the game items and invite each player to choose one. Tell kids these items are pretend bananas. Set the *kitchen timer* at one end of the playing area. Choose two kids to be the Zoo Keepers and have them set their "bananas" at the opposite end of the playing area from the timer.

INSIDE TIP

Young children really go "ape" for this game. Play Monkey Maze to enrich your lessons on Noah's ark.

Say: **The Zoo Keepers are in a cage full of playful "Monkeys." When I say, "Monkey madness," the Monkeys will create a goofy obstacle course by touching their game items (or bananas) together. Monkeys can sit or stand or lay down or stretch their arms out or whatever. The Monkeys must freeze in place that way. I'll start the timer and say "go." Then the Zoo Keepers must make their way through the maze of Monkeys by crawling under Monkeys' arms or stepping over the Monkeys to collect all of the bananas before time runs out. When time's up, Monkeys can toss their bananas in the air and yell "EEEK!"**

Set the timer for one minute or less. Have the Monkeys encourage the Zoo Keepers by squeaking, "Eek, eek" as the Zoo Keepers pass. At the end of the first round, choose two new Zoo Keepers. You may wish to subtract five seconds each round the Zoo Keepers make it through the maze in time.

HOP'N'POP

GET READY...

GROUP SIZE: Any
BEST FOR GRADES: 2-6
PLAYING TIME: 10 minutes
ENERGY LEVEL: High
ITEMS NEEDED: The *balloons* and the *masking tape*

GET SET...

OBJECT OF THE GAME: Keep hoppin' to save your *balloon* from poppin'.

GO!

DIRECTIONS: Hand each child a *balloon* to blow up and tie off. Offer help to children who may not be able to tie their own *balloons*. Hand everyone a 10-inch piece of *masking tape*. Direct kids to tape one end of the *masking tape* to the knot on the *balloon* and the other end to their shoelace or shoe. Fold the tape in half between the shoe and *balloon* so the tape sticks together.

Say: **We're going to get things hopping with this game. When I clap my hands, start hoppin' and poppin'** *balloons* **by stepping on them—but don't let your own** *balloon* **pop! If your** *balloon* **pops, sit down and help cheer the rest of the players on.**

Continue until one player's *balloon* is left unpopped. That player may line up first for drinks or hand out more *balloons* and *masking tape* for another round.

ROCK 'N' ROLL RELAY

GROUP SIZE: 6 or more
BEST FOR GRADES: 4-6
PLAYING TIME: 15 minutes
ENERGY LEVEL: High
ITEMS NEEDED: 2 *jump-ropes*, 2 *bandannas*, and 2 *Ping-Pong balls*

GET SET...

OBJECT OF THE GAME: Help your group roll to the finish line first.

GO!

DIRECTIONS: Establish a starting line by laying the *jump-ropes* at one end of the playing area. Lay the *bandannas* at the opposite end as a finish line. Have kids form two groups of "Rollers." Show Rollers how to line up side by side on their hands and knees. Hand the last player in each line a *Ping-Pong ball*.

Say: **Let's get this game rolling, shall we? When I say, "Rock 'n' roll," the last person in each line will lay on his or her side and roll across the backs of the Rollers. When you get to the front of the line, roll the** *Ping-Pong ball* **under-**

neath the Rollers to the last person. Then that player will get rolling. Keep rockin' and rollin' until your group crosses the finish line.

Play the game again but this time have the players crawl under the Rollers, instead of rolling across their backs.

PAT THE CAT

GET READY...

GROUP SIZE: Any
BEST FOR GRADES: K-2
PLAYING TIME: 15 minutes
ENERGY LEVEL: Low
ITEMS NEEDED: 2 *bandannas* and a *jump-rope*

GET SET...

OBJECT OF THE GAME: Pat the Cat without getting caught.

GO!

DIRECTIONS: Place a chair in front of the group. Choose one player to be the "Cat" and sit in the chair. Blindfold the Cat with one *bandanna* and then place the other *bandanna* on the Cat's head. Direct the other players to sit a few feet in front of the Cat. Place the *jump-rope* in a circle a few feet away from the Cat as the "mouse hole."

> **INSIDE TIP**
>
> For an extra challenge, have the Cat guess who snatched the *bandanna!*

Say: **It's fun to pat a cat, but in this game you have to be fast, too. I'll secretly point to someone to sneak up and pat the Cat by snatching the *bandanna*. If you're tagged by the Cat, you turn into a mouse and must sit in the mouse hole. If you snatch the *bandanna* without getting tagged, you become the next Cat.**

Play until everyone has had a chance to be the Cat.

COOL PASS-OFFS

⚡ GET READY...

GROUP SIZE: Any
BEST FOR GRADES: K-6
PLAYING TIME: 10-15 minutes
ENERGY LEVEL: Medium
ITEMS NEEDED: The *balloons* and water

⚡ GET SET...

OBJECT OF THE GAME: Keep your *balloon* from popping as you cool off with watery fun.

⚡ GO!

DIRECTIONS: This game is best played on a hot summer day. Be sure kids are wearing swimsuits or other clothes that can get wet.

Fill two *balloons* with water for each child. Form pairs and instruct them to line up facing each other a foot apart. Hand each partner on one side of the line a water *balloon* and then set the rest of the water *balloons* aside.

Say: **When I clap, toss the *balloons* to your partners. If the *balloons* are caught without popping, both partners take one step backward. Then I'll clap again, and you can toss your *balloons* back. We'll see who can catch their *balloons* the longest.**

After one round, play another "cool" game with the remainder of the water *balloons*. Have kids stand in a circle. Say: **When I say, "Green light," begin passing two water *balloons* in opposite directions. When I say, "Red light," stop passing the *balloons*. Whoever has a *balloon* must sit on the *balloon* and pop it. Then those people sit in the center of the circle.** Have kids begin passing two more *balloons*. Continue until all the water *balloons* have been popped.

DODGE-PODGE

⚡ GET READY...

GROUP SIZE: 9 or more
BEST FOR GRADES: 3-6
PLAYING TIME: 15 minutes
ENERGY LEVEL: High
ITEMS NEEDED: The *masking tape* and the *playground ball*

GET SET...

OBJECT OF THE GAME: Play cooperatively and tag opponents to join your group.

GO!

DIRECTIONS: Establish a center line by placing a strip of *masking tape* down the middle of the playing area. (If you're playing outside, use the *jump-ropes* for a center line.) Form two groups on either side of the center line and have each group number off by threes. Assign the following roles for each number:

- ones can only catch the ball,
- twos can only throw the ball, and
- threes can only pick up the ball.

Say: **This game is played just like Dodge Ball, except you'll have to work together to tag your opponents with the ball. Each member of your group can only do what his or her number allows. If you're a one, you may only catch the ball; if you're a two, you may only throw the ball; and if you're a three, you may only pick up the ball. If you're tagged, you must join the other group.**

Have kids continue playing until there's only one person left on a side. Remind kids of their roles until they get the hang of the game. Play the game again but renumber the kids to play new roles.

PUPPY-DOG TAILS

GET READY...

GROUP SIZE: 6 or more
BEST FOR GRADES: K-4
PLAYING TIME: 15 minutes
ENERGY LEVEL: High
ITEMS NEEDED: 2 *bandannas*

GET SET...

OBJECT OF THE GAME: Be the first puppy to chase and snatch its opponents' tail.

GO!

DIRECTIONS: Form two groups or "puppies." Have the puppies stand in a line. The first person in line is the "head." Have each child hold the waist of the person in front of him or her.

Hand the last person in each puppy line a *bandanna* to tuck into his or her waistband or belt so it hangs down like a tail. (If a child isn't wearing a belt or doesn't have a waistband, have him or her hold the *bandanna* in back like a tail.)

INSIDE TIP

For a different game, form one long puppy and have the "head" chase the "tail" to snatch the *bandanna*. Encourage the tail to dodge and keep away from the puppy's head.

Say: **I can see you're puppies that are ready to play! When I say, "Chase 'em!" the head of each puppy will lead you in a chase to try and snatch the other dog's tail. Don't let go of the person in front of you or your puppy is out!**

Have children play until the "tail" of one puppy is snatched and then form new puppies and play again.

TRUE OR FALSE

GET READY...

GROUP SIZE: Any
BEST FOR GRADES: 1-6
PLAYING TIME: 10 minutes
ENERGY LEVEL: Medium
ITEMS NEEDED: 2 *jump-ropes* and a *bandanna*

GET SET...

OBJECT OF THE GAME: Help your group chase and capture your opponents before they reach their Safety Zone.

GO!

DIRECTIONS: Lay the *jump-ropes* 30 feet apart outside or in a gymnasium. Tell kids the areas behind the *jump-ropes* are the Safety Zones. Set the *bandanna* between the *jump-ropes*. Form two groups: the True and the False. Have groups line up facing each other on opposite sides of the *bandanna*.

Say: **We're going to play a great chase game of True and False. I'll tell you a sentence. If it's true, the True group chases the False group to their Safety Zone. But if the sentence is false, the False group chases the Trues to their Safety Zone. Once in your Safety Zone, you can't be tagged. But if you're tagged while running, you must join the other group.**

INSIDE TIP

This is a wonderful game to use when reviewing or reinforcing Bible stories and characters. Use statements such as "Moses marched around the walls of Jericho" or "Mary and Joseph took baby Jesus to Egypt."

Use the following sentences, then make up more of your own. Let kids take turns calling out true and false sentences.

- **The sky is purple.** (F)
- **All kids love to eat spinach.** (F)
- **Fish live under water.** (T)
- **There are 60 seconds in one minute.** (T)
- **Six plus three take away two equals five.** (F)

Play for 10 minutes or until there are only a few kids on one side.

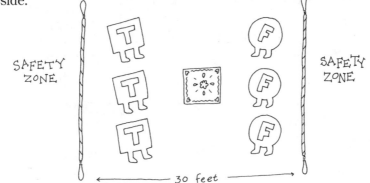

SAFETY ZONE   SAFETY ZONE

← 30 feet →

Moon Balloon

⚡ Get Ready...

GROUP SIZE: Any
BEST FOR GRADES: K-6
PLAYING TIME: 15 minutes
ENERGY LEVEL: Medium
ITEMS NEEDED: A *jump-rope* and the *balloon*s

⚡ Get Set...

OBJECT OF THE GAME: Help your group of astronauts be the first on the moon using rocket-ship *balloon*s.

⚡ Go!

DIRECTIONS: Place the *jump-rope* in a circle at one end of the playing area as the "moon." Form two groups of "astronauts" and have them line up at the opposite end of the room from the moon. Hand each astronaut a *balloon*.

Say: **Each astronaut is holding a *balloon* rocket ship. When I say "Blastoff!" the first astronaut will blow up his or her rocket ship, then let it go. The next astronaut in the group will run to the place the rocket ship landed and blow up his or her *balloon* rocket ship and let it go. Continue taking turns launching your rocket ships until you make it to the moon.**

Rocket ships don't need to land directly inside the circle moon but must be even with or travel beyond the moon for a successful moon landing!

SNEAK PEEK

GET READY...

GROUP SIZE: Any
BEST FOR GRADES: K-4
PLAYING TIME: 15 minutes
ENERGY LEVEL: Medium
ITEMS NEEDED: A *jump-rope*, a *bandanna*, and the *kitchen timer*

GET SET...

OBJECT OF THE GAME: Sneak your way forward and be the first to snatch the *bandanna*.

GO!

DIRECTIONS: Place the *jump-rope* at one end of the playing area as the starting line. Set the *bandanna* at the opposite end. Choose one child to be the "Sneaky Peeker" and have him or her stand behind the *bandanna*. Have other kids line up on the *jump-rope*.

Say: **Are you as quiet as a mouse? as fast as a rabbit? as sneaky as a fox? You'll need to be in this game! I'll start the timer. When the Sneaky Peeker turns his or her back and says "Sneak!" begin inching your way toward the *bandanna*. But when the Sneaky Peeker says "Peek!" freeze in place, or you'll have to go back to the starting line and begin again. The first one to sneak up and snatch the *bandanna* before time runs out becomes the next Sneaky Peeker.**

> **INSIDE TIP**
> Most older children love this age-old classic of Stop and Go. For an extra challenge, have kids move in different ways such as hopping or inching along on their bottoms.

CROCODILE CRAWL

GET READY...

GROUP SIZE: 6 or more
BEST FOR GRADES: K-3
PLAYING TIME: 10 minutes
ENERGY LEVEL: Medium
ITEMS NEEDED: 2 *jump-ropes*, 2 *bandannas*, 6 *cups*, and 6 *disks*

GET SET...

OBJECT OF THE GAME: Be part of a creepy, crawly crocodile and collect items on your way to the swamp.

Go!

DIRECTIONS: Establish start and finish lines at opposite ends of the playing area using the *jump-ropes* and *bandannas*. Scatter six *cups* and six *disks* between the start and finish lines. Instruct kids to form three groups or "crocodiles" and line up single file behind the starting line. Tell kids that the first person in each line is the crocodile's "head." Have kids squat and hold the shoulders of the person in front of them.

Say: **Look at the crawly crocodiles here today! I know you miss your swamp and want to go there for a swim. When I say "go," begin creeping your way to the finish-line swamp, but along the way your crocodile must pick up two *cups* and two *disks*. Any part of the crocodile may pick up these items, not just the head. When you've collected your items, crawl to the swamp and roll over on your backs for a crocodile tickle.**

Begin the game, then tickle the tummies of each crocodile that crosses the finish line. Form new crocodiles and play again.

SCOOT FOR THE LOOT

GET READY...

GROUP SIZE: 8 or more
BEST FOR GRADES: K-6
PLAYING TIME: 15 minutes
ENERGY LEVEL: Medium
ITEMS NEEDED: The *masking tape*, a *bandanna*, and the *color* and *number cubes*

GET SET...

OBJECT OF THE GAME: Remember your secret color and number, then be the first to grab the "loot."

GO!

> **INSIDE TIP**
>
> For an extra challenge with older kids, make the square larger and have them scoot without using their hands.

DIRECTIONS: Make a 5-foot *masking tape* square on the floor and place the *bandanna* in the center of it. Secretly assign each child a color (red, yellow, green, or blue) and a number from one to four. Tell kids they'll need to remember both their colors and numbers. Invite kids to sit around the *masking tape* square.

Say: **Everyone knows how to scoot. Let's try it once. Scoot to the center of the square.** Pause as kids scoot on their bottoms to the center and back. **In this game, you'll scoot for the "loot," the *bandanna,* in the center of the square. I'll roll the *color* and *number cubes* and call out the color and number rolled. Anyone with that color and number must scoot to the center of the square and be the first to grab the loot. Then that player becomes the next Roller.**

Play until everyone has had a chance to be the Roller.

OVER, UNDER, SIDEWAYS, DOWN

GET READY...

GROUP SIZE: 6 or more
BEST FOR GRADES: 2-6
PLAYING TIME: 15 minutes
ENERGY LEVEL: High
ITEMS NEEDED: The *foam* or *playground ball*, a *disk*, a *jump-rope*, and the *kitchen timer*

GET SET...

OBJECT OF THE GAME: Work together to beat the clock in this wacky passing game.

GO!

DIRECTIONS: Have kids stand single file. Set the *kitchen timer* where everyone can see it, such as on a chair or a table.

Say: **We'll try to beat the clock in this game by passing three items in three different ways. We'll pass the ball over our heads, the *disk* under our knees, and the *jump-rope* sideways around our waists. When the last person in line receives an item, set the item down. When all the items have been passed, sit down quickly.**

Start the timer. Continue until everyone is sitting down and then stop the timer. On the next round, have kids scramble the order in which they're standing and try for a faster time.

> **iNSIDE TiP**
>
> Have older kids try passing a pair of items at once. Use both balls for over, two *disks* for under, and two *jump-ropes* for sideways. You can also play this "double pass" game with two groups.

STEPPING STONES

GET READY...

GROUP SIZE: Any
BEST FOR GRADES: K-4
PLAYING TIME: 10 minutes
ENERGY LEVEL: Medium
ITEMS NEEDED: 2 *jump-ropes*, 3 *cups*, and 6 *disks*

GET SET...

OBJECT OF THE GAME: Help your partner walk on stepping stones to the finish line.

GO!

DIRECTIONS: Establish start and finish lines at opposite ends of the playing area using the *jump-ropes*. Set the *cups* behind the finish line.

Direct kids to find partners. (If there's an uneven number of children, someone can go twice or you may be someone's part-

ner.) Have partners stand behind the starting line. Hand
each pair two *disks*. Have partners decide who will be the
Stepper and who will be the Stone Layer.

INSIDE TIP

This is a good
game to reinforce
the concept of fol-
lowing Jesus and
letting Jesus guide
our steps in life.

Say: **Stepping stones help you get safely from one
place to the next. In this game, the Steppers cannot
touch the ground but must walk on the stepping
stones, or *disks*, that the Stone Layer sets down.
You'll walk on the stepping stones to the finish line,
pick up a *cup*, then switch places for the return trip to the
starting line. The next pair will take the *cup* to the finish
line and set it down. Let's practice stepping on the stones.**

Demonstrate how to set down a *disk* and then have the Stepper
stand on that *disk* as you set down another. When the Stepper lifts
his or her first foot, pick up the *disk* and set it down again. Let kids
have a few moments to practice, then begin the game. Continue
playing until all the partners have had a chance to be Steppers
and Stone Layers.

ATOMS AND MOLECULES

GET READY...

GROUP SIZE: 6 or more
BEST FOR GRADES: K-6
PLAYING TIME: 15 minutes
ENERGY LEVEL: Medium
ITEMS NEEDED: 6 *disks* and the
kitchen timer

GET SET...

OBJECT OF THE GAME: Travel in your "molecule" and collect the most *disks* before time runs out.

GO!

INSIDE TIP

For an extra chal-
lenge, have mem-
bers of each Mol-
ecule stand with
their backs facing
inward and lock
arms!

DIRECTIONS: Scatter the six *disks* around the playing
area. Have kids form groups of three to five "Molecules."
Direct Molecules to hold hands and form circles. Then
have each Molecule choose an "Atom" to stand in the
center.

Say: **Let's get a little atomic power moving today!
You're all groups of Molecules and have Atoms standing in
your centers. The Molecule's job is to protect its Atom from
being tagged by another Molecule while it travels the play-**

ing field in search of power *disks* to pick up. The Atom is the only part of your Molecule allowed to pick up power *disks*. I'll start the timer, and you'll have one minute to pick up as many power *disks* as you can. If your Atom is tagged by another Molecule, your entire Molecule must sit down.

Start the timer and after one minute call "stop." The Molecule with the most *disks* gets to scatter the disks for the second round.

BOUNCING BAUBLES

GET READY...

GROUP SIZE: 8 or more
BEST FOR GRADES: K-6
PLAYING TIME: 15 minutes
ENERGY LEVEL: Medium
ITEMS NEEDED: 2 *bandannas*, 6 *disks*, 6 *cups*, 2 *Ping-Pong balls*, and the *color* and *number cubes*

GET SET...

OBJECT OF THE GAME: Form an assembly line and vault your pile of "baubles" from one end to the other.

GO!

DIRECTIONS: Form two groups and hand each the following items: a *bandanna*, three *disks*, three *cups*, a *Ping-Pong ball*, and a *cube*. Tell each group to choose a Tosser and a Catcher and then form a line. Instruct the Tosser to stand a foot from the end of the line and the Catcher a foot in front of the line. Have the kids in between hold the edges of the *bandanna*. Place the rest of the "baubles" beside the Tosser.

Say: **You have a lot of pretty baubles that must go from the end of your line to the front, and you all have an impor-**

tant role in getting them there! When I say "go," the Tosser will toss a bauble to the players with the *bandanna*. Those players will bounce the bauble on the *bandanna* and send it to the Catcher who catches the bauble and sets it down. We'll see which group is the fastest bauble bouncer!

Repeat the game a few times mixing up players each round. Try having Tossers toss two baubles at once or begin passing a second bauble before the first is "home."

WHIPLASH

GET READY...

GROUP SIZE: Any
BEST FOR GRADES: 3-6
PLAYING TIME: 15 minutes
ENERGY LEVEL: High
ITEMS NEEDED: 2 *disks*, 2 *jump-ropes*, and 2 *bandannas*

GET SET...

OBJECT OF THE GAME: Run to collect your group members, then whip to the *disk* and snatch it up!

GO!

DIRECTIONS: Place two *disks* in the center of the playing area. Form two groups. Hand one person a *jump-rope* and one person a *bandanna* in each group.

Say: **A whiplash moves back and forth very quickly. You're going to become a whiplash in a moment. The players with the *jump-ropes* will say, "One, two, hip, hop, three, four, now stop!" You'll run and scatter until they say "stop!" Then freeze in place. The players with the *jump-ropes* will run to gather their groups. The first player "collected" in each group will hold onto the end of the *jump-rope*. Then the next player will hold onto the hand of the last player collected. When your whole group is together, run to the *disks*, but only the player holding the *bandanna* may pick up a *disk*.**

Play until one group has picked up a *disk* and then form new groups and play again.

> ## INSIDE TIP
>
> For extra excitement with older kids, use only one *disk*. Or play the game without *disks* and create a jumbo whip to race around the playing area.

CROSS THE SEA

GET READY...

GROUP SIZE: Any
BEST FOR GRADES: 2-6
PLAYING TIME: 10 minutes
ENERGY LEVEL: Medium
ITEMS NEEDED: The *jump-ropes* and 6 *disks*

GET SET...

OBJECT OF THE GAME: Toss the *disks* over the sea and then travel in odd ways to rescue them.

Go!

DIRECTIONS: This game is best played outdoors. Lay the *jump-ropes* across the center of the playing area as the "sea." Have kids stand 15 feet from the sea. Hand six kids each a *disk*.

iNSiDE TiP

Add more challenge by having kids rescue the *disks* in pairs with their arms locked.

Say: **This is a rescue game. We'll all count, "one, two, three." On the count of three, the players with the *disks* will throw them across the sea like a Frisbee. Then we'll say, "Cross the sea and rescue me," and walk heel to toe to rescue the *disks* that flew out to sea. Whoever gets a *disk* will throw it next time.**

If any *disks* fail to sail across the sea, don't rescue them until the other *disks* have been grabbed. Play until everyone has had a turn to throw a *disk*. Vary the mode of travel such as hopping, crawling, somersaulting, or skipping to rescue the *disks*.

GiFT GiVER

GET READY...

GROUP SIZE: Any
BEST FOR GRADES: K-3
PLAYING TIME: 10 minutes
ENERGY LEVEL: Low
ITEMS NEEDED: 6 *disks*

GET SET...

OBJECT OF THE GAME: Guess who gave you a "gift" and be the next Giver.

Go!

DIRECTIONS: Gather kids in a group on the floor. Hand six kids each a *disk*. If your group is small, use only two or three *disks*.

Say: **I've just handed pretend gifts to six Givers. In a moment you'll hide your eyes and put one of your hands in the air. The Givers will sneak around the room and each place a gift in someone's hand. When we say, "Five, four, three, two, guess who gave a gift to you!" open your eyes. Then you'll have one try to guess who gave you the gift. If you're right, you're the next Giver.**

Play until everyone's had a chance to be a Giver.

UPSIDE-DOWNSIDE

GET READY...

GROUP SIZE: Any
BEST FOR GRADES: K-4
PLAYING TIME: 10 minutes
ENERGY LEVEL: High
ITEMS NEEDED: 2 *rulers* and 6 *cups*

GET SET...

OBJECT OF THE GAME: Take turns racing to turn your *cups* upside down and then right-side up.

Go!

DIRECTIONS: Lay the *rulers* at one end of the playing area as two starting lines. Place three *cups* in a row beginning five feet from each starting line. Be sure there are five feet between the *cups* in each row. Form two groups and have players huddle to decide how they'll travel. For example, they may choose to run, walk heel to toe, crawl, or hop on one foot. Tell them that each person in their group must choose a different way to travel. Then have players line up single file behind their starting lines.

Say: **In this game you'll travel in your special way to the cups. The first players will turn their three cups upside down. Then they'll run back and sit down. The next players will travel in their special ways and set the cups right-side up. We'll continue until everyone is sitting down.**

Begin the relay by saying "go." The first group sitting down gets to line up first for drinks of water.

HUMAN JACKS

GET READY...

GROUP SIZE: 6 or more
BEST FOR GRADES: K-3
PLAYING TIME: 15 minutes
ENERGY LEVEL: High
ITEM NEEDED: The *playground ball*

GET SET...

OBJECT OF THE GAME: Play a giant game of Jacks and make number groups.

GO!

DIRECTIONS: Stand in a circle. Choose one child to be the Tosser and hand him or her the *playground ball*.

INSIDE TIP

This game is also fun when you use items from the game bag. Set a variety of items near the Tosser and when a number is called, have kids run to assemble the number of items called.

Say: **This game is played like Jacks, only we're using people instead of jacks. The Tosser will toss the ball high in the air and begin by calling out "one-sies." You must form groups of one before the Tosser catches the ball. Then the Tosser will toss the ball again and say "twosies." Run to form groups of two before he or she catches the ball. If you can't find a group before the Tosser catches the ball, sit down until he or she calls the next group number.**

We'll continue until everyone forms one large group.

Continue playing until each child has been the Tosser.

SWIRLIN' SAM

GET READY...

GROUP SIZE: Any
BEST FOR GRADES: K-2
PLAYING TIME: 10 minutes
ENERGY LEVEL: High
ITEMS NEEDED: 2 *jump-ropes*

GET SET...

OBJECT OF THE GAME: Jump over the swirling ropes and sing your favorite songs.

Go!

DIRECTIONS: Tie the *jump-ropes* together to make one long rope. Choose someone to be Swirlin' Sam and hand him or her the *jump-rope*.

Say: **Swirlin' Sam is going to get things jumping! Sam will twirl the *jump-rope* around in a low circle while we jump over the rope. As we jump, we'll repeat a counting verse. Then we'll see how many jumps we can make before someone misses. When someone misses, we'll choose a new Swirlin' Sam.**

As kids jump over the rope, repeat the following rhyme:

Blue-berry, straw-berry, huckle-berry-boo.
How many jumps can we do?
(Begin counting jumps.)

When someone misses, choose a new Swirlin' Sam and begin again. Use other *jump-rope* chants or sing songs as kids jump.

> ### INSIDE TIP
> Kids love to jump rope! Leave the ropes tied together and jump in the traditional way with two kids twirling the rope. Use the same rhyme and let kids try to better their own "jumping score" with each turn.

FORE BY FOUR

GET READY...

GROUP SIZE: Up to 12
BEST FOR GRADES: 4-6
PLAYING TIME: 15 minutes
ENERGY LEVEL: Medium
ITEMS NEEDED: 6 *cups* and 2 *Ping-Pong balls*

GET SET...

OBJECT OF THE GAME: Play a round of goofy golf and be the foursome with the least number of strokes.

GO!

DIRECTIONS: Put six *cups* on their sides around the playing area. Invite kids to form foursomes and choose one person to be the Driver, one to be the Putter, and two kids to be the Hitters. (If you have a small group, partners can double up by being a Driver/Hitter and a Putter/Hitter. If your group is larger than eight, have extra kids be Hitters.) Hand each group a *Ping-Pong ball*. Gather kids at one end of the playing area.

Say: **It's a great day for a game of goofy golf. There are six cups or "holes" in our goofy golf course. You'll play each hole and work in your groups to get the lowest score. The Drivers kick the *Ping-Pong balls* first each time and aim toward any *cup*. Then the Hitters each take a turn kicking the ball closer to the *cup*. Finally, the Putters can gently tap the ball into the *cup* with their feet. No hands allowed in this game! Then begin again and aim toward another *cup*. Keep track of your kicks or "strokes." Then we'll see who has the lowest number at the end of six holes.**

When everyone has finished the course, let the group with the lowest score hand out special 19th-hole treats such as marshmallow "golf balls" or Life Savers "holes."

FROGS ON THE LiLY PADS

GET READY...

GROUP SIZE: Any
BEST FOR GRADES: K-3
PLAYING TIME: 10 minutes
ENERGY LEVEL: High
ITEMS NEEDED: 6 *disks* and the *color* and *number cubes*

GET SET...

OBJECT OF THE GAME: Be leapin' frogs and capture a lily pad.

GO!

DIRECTIONS: Place the *disks* at one end of the playing area as "lily pads." Gather kids at the opposite end and have them team up with a friend. Assign each pair a color (red, yellow, green, or blue).

Say: **You're frogs hopping to lily pads. I'll roll the** *color* **and** *number cubes.* **If your color is rolled, you and your froggy partner will leapfrog the number of times rolled on the** *number cube.* **For example, if I roll yellow and the #3, the yellow frog pairs will leapfrog three times toward the lily pads. When you reach a lily pad, sit on it. We'll play until all the lily pads are captured.**

If your group is smaller than 12, use fewer lily pads. You may also play this game with individual hopping frogs!

FREEZE BALL

GET READY...

GROUP SIZE: Any
BEST FOR GRADES: K-6
PLAYING TIME: 15 minutes
ENERGY LEVEL: High
ITEM NEEDED: The *playground ball*

GET SET...

OBJECT OF THE GAME: Don't get tagged by the ball while you're frozen in place.

Go!

DIRECTIONS: This game is best when played outdoors or in a gymnasium. Have kids stand in the center of the playing area. Hand one player the *playground ball* and designate this player as "Frosty."

> **iNSiDE TiP**
>
> For younger kids or when you want to play this game indoors, have Frosty roll the ball.

Say: **In this game, Frosty will try to turn you into freezing ice cubes. When Frosty tosses the ball in the air, run and scatter. But when Frosty catches the ball and shouts "Freeze!" you must stop. Then Frosty will take three giant steps toward any player and throw the ball waist level or below. You may stoop or swivel to dodge the ball, but one foot must remain frozen in place. If you catch the ball, you become the next Frosty. If you're tagged, you become an ice cube and must sit down. We'll play until there's only one person who's not an ice cube.**

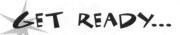

SWiTCH-o, CHANGE-o

GET READY...

GROUP SIZE: At least 7
BEST FOR GRADES: K-6
PLAYING TIME: 10 minutes
ENERGY LEVEL: High
ITEM NEEDED: The *color cube*

GET SET...

OBJECT OF THE GAME: Hurry to switch places but don't get caught without a spot!

GO!

DIRECTIONS: Have kids sit in a large circle and assign each player a color (red, yellow, green, or blue). Instruct kids to remember their colors. Choose someone to be "It" and squat in the center of the circle holding the *color cube*.

> **iNSiDE TiP**
>
> Older kids enjoy spreading out rather than playing in a circle. Let older kids run to switch places but tell them to be careful of collisions.

Say: **You've got to be a quick-change artist in this game. It will roll the *color cube* and call out the color rolled. All the players with that color must stand up and hop to change places with someone else of that color. It will try to get into one of the empty spots, too, so you'll have to switch-o, change-o quickly! The player caught without a place becomes It.**

Vary the way kids change places such as skipping, inching on their bottoms, or walking backward. Continue playing until each person has been It and rolled the *color cube*.

KANGAROO HOP

GET READY...

GROUP SIZE: Any
BEST FOR GRADES: K-2
PLAYING TIME: 10 minutes
ENERGY LEVEL: High
ITEMS NEEDED: 2 *jump-ropes*, 2 *bandannas*, the *playground ball*, and the *foam ball*

GET SET...

OBJECT OF THE GAME: Be the first group of hopping kangaroos to travel to the zoo and back.

GO!

DIRECTIONS: Establish start and finish lines by laying the *jump-ropes* 20 feet apart or at opposite ends of the playing area. Place the two *bandannas* behind the finish line. Have kids form two groups of "kangaroos" and direct them to stand in single file lines behind the starting line. Hand the first kangaroo in each group a ball.

Say: **I see lots of kangaroos ready for a good hop. When I say "go," the first kangaroos will place the balls between their knees, hop to the zoo or finish line, and pick up the *bandannas*. Then hop back to your group and hand the ball and the *bandanna* to the next kangaroo. We'll keep things hopping until all the kangaroos have gone to the zoo and back.**

SATELLITE SPIN

GET READY...

GROUP SIZE: Any
BEST FOR GRADES: K-6
PLAYING TIME: 10 minutes
ENERGY LEVEL: Medium
ITEM NEEDED: A *disk*

GET SET...

OBJECT OF THE GAME: Keep the satellite in orbit by continually spinning it.

GO!

DIRECTIONS: Have kids sit in a circle and number off so that each child has a different number. (If your group is very large, form two circles and use two *disks* to play.) Be sure to tell kids what the number span is, such as one through eight or one through 14. Instruct them to remember their numbers.

Say: **This *disk* is a "satellite" and our mission is to keep it in orbit. I'll launch the satellite by giving it a spin. Then I'll call out a number from one to** (whatever your span is)**. The player with that number must run to the center and give the satellite another spin before it stops. Then he or she can call out another number. We'll see how long we can keep the satellite in orbit.**

Be sure everyone has a chance to spin the satellite at least once. For an extra challenge with older groups, use multiple *disks* and keep them all spinning!

FiRefLiES AND FiRE- FiGHTERS

GET READY...

GROUP SIZE: Up to 20
BEST FOR GRADES: K-6
PLAYING TIME: 15 minutes
ENERGY LEVEL: High
ITEMS NEEDED: 6 *cups*, the *kitchen timer*, and water

GET SET...

OBJECT OF THE GAME: Tag the fireflies before time runs out and their fires are quenched.

Go!

DIRECTIONS: This is a summer game and should be played outside when kids are dressed in swimsuits or old clothes. Fill six *cups* with water. Form two groups and designate one group as the Taggers. Instruct the other group to form pairs and choose which partners will be the Fireflies and which will be the Firefighters. Hand each Firefighter a *cup* of water.

iNSiDE TiP

This is a great game to play at a picnic gathering where most adults will love to join in the action.

Say: **This is a hot game! I'll turn over the timer and say "Fire!" The Taggers will run to tag Fireflies. If any Fireflies are tagged, they must sit down until a** Firefighter pours water on them. The Firefly is then free to fly again. If a Firefighter runs out of water, he or she must sit down. Taggers will try to capture all the Fireflies before time runs out or the water runs dry.

After you've played, refill the *cups* and play again. Play until everyone has been a Firefly.

ZiGZAG-ZALLy

GET READY...

GROUP SIZE: 10 or more
BEST FOR GRADES: 3-6
PLAYING TIME: 10 minutes
ENERGY LEVEL: Low
ITEMS NEEDED: The *playground ball* and the *foam ball*

GET SET...

OBJECT OF THE GAME: To be the first group to toss your ball zigzag up and down the line.

Go!

DIRECTIONS: Have kids number off by twos. Direct groups to stand in two lines, about three feet apart. Have each player face a member of the other group. Hand a ball to the player standing at the end of each line.

Say: **This is a zany zigzag game. You'll be tossing the balls in zigzag fashion to your group members. When I say "go," the first person in each line will** toss the ball diagonally to the group member opposite him or her. The first players catching the balls will say "zig," then the second players will say "zag," and the next will say "zally," and so on down the line. Then toss the ball back up the line. The group who zigzag-zallys up and down the line first chooses the next game.

> ### INSIDE TIP
> For older kids, decide on how many zigzag-zallys must be completed for a game. Try using *balloons* for a different twist.

CRAZY CRICKETS

GET READY...

GROUP SIZE: Any
BEST FOR GRADES: K-6
PLAYING TIME: 15 minutes
ENERGY LEVEL: Medium
ITEMS NEEDED: The *masking tape* and the *playground ball*

GET SET...

OBJECT OF THE GAME: Jump over the ball before you get tagged.

GO!

DIRECTIONS: Use the *masking tape* to make a 10-foot diameter circle on the floor. Then divide the circle into four equal sections with *masking tape* lines.

Choose two kids to be Rollers and have them stand on opposite sides of the circle. Hand one of the Rollers the *playground ball*. Direct the rest of the kids, or "crickets," to stand in the quarter sections of the circle. Tell them they must remain in those sections for the entire game.

Say: **Crickets are high jumpers, especially in this game. The Rollers will roll the ball back and forth across the circle. Jump over the ball before it tags you. If you're tagged, you become a Roller and help tag other crickets. Remember, you must stay in your section of the circle! We'll play until there's only one cricket left.**

Older kids enjoy this game as much as younger ones. Add an extra challenge by playing with two balls and let the crickets roam the entire circle to dodge the balls.

WHALE TAIL

GET READY...

GROUP SIZE: Any
BEST FOR GRADES: K-2
PLAYING TIME: 15 minutes
ENERGY LEVEL: Low
ITEM NEEDED: A *bandanna*

GET SET...

OBJECT OF THE GAME: Don't get caught snatching the whale's tail.

Go!

DIRECTIONS: Choose a child to be the "Whale" and sit with his or her back to the group. Lay the *bandanna* behind the Whale.

Say: **We can be secret whale-tail snatchers. I'll point to someone to sneak up and silently snatch the Whale's tail. When he or she returns, we'll all hide our hands in our laps. We'll try to fool the** Whale so he or she won't know who has the tail. Then we'll say, "Whopping Whale, who has your tail?" The Whale will have two chances to find the missing tail. If the Whale guesses correctly, the snatcher becomes the next Whale. If the Whale doesn't find the tail, we'll play again, and the person who had the tail may point to the next tail snatcher.

Continue playing until each child has snatched the tail at least once.

> **INSIDE TIP**
>
> If you have a large group of kids, play a variation called Fish Fins. Use two *bandannas* as fins and have two snatchers.

HURRICANE

GET READY...

GROUP SIZE: Any
BEST FOR GRADES: K-6
PLAYING TIME: 15 minutes
ENERGY LEVEL: Medium
ITEMS NEEDED: The *masking tape* and the *balloons*

GET SET...

OBJECT OF THE GAME: Huff 'n' puff 'n' blow the *balloon* to another group before it touches the floor.

Go!

DIRECTIONS: Make a 5-foot diameter circle on the floor with *masking tape*. Then divide the circle into thirds with *masking tape* lines. Have kids number off by threes. Direct each group to stand in one section of the circle with their hands behind their backs. Inform kids that they'll remain in these sections for the entire game. To promote game spirit, encourage each group to create a name for themselves such as the Silver Streaks or the Jumping Jacks. Blow up and tie off a few *balloons* and then set them aside.

Say: **Hurricanes really blow, and that's what we'll do in this game. I'll toss a *balloon* in the center of the circle. You'll work with your groups to blow the *balloon* to someone else's area of the circle. Don't let the *balloon* touch the floor in your section. And no hands allowed—just lots of huffs 'n' puffs!**

Play until the *balloon* touches the floor. Then play again using two *balloons*. End game time by keeping three *balloons* in play. You may wish to add an extra challenge by having players kneel!

STEAL THE DEAL

GET READY...

GROUP SIZE: Any
BEST FOR GRADES: K-2
PLAYING TIME: 15 minutes
ENERGY LEVEL: Low
ITEMS NEEDED: The *color cube*, the *playground ball*, the *kitchen timer*, and 1 less item than there are kids

GET SET...

OBJECT OF THE GAME: Be the player with the *color cube* when time runs out.

GO!

DIRECTIONS: Have kids sit in a circle with their legs folded and their knees touching the people on either side to create a solid circle. Hand one child the *color cube* and give the rest of the kids each a game item. Tell them to set their items in front of them on the floor.

Say: **In this game you'll try to bowl over items and take them. I'll set the timer, and then we'll take turns rolling the ball around the circle. If you hit someone's item, he or she must give it to you to set in front of you. You may even hit two or three things with one roll! When the time runs out, the person with the *color cube* begins the next game.**

SAVE THE KiNG OR QUEEN!

GET READY...

GROUP SIZE: 10 or more
BEST FOR GRADES: 3-6
PLAYING TIME: 20 minutes
ENERGY LEVEL: High
ITEMS NEEDED: 2 *jump-ropes* and 2 *bandannas*

GET SET...

OBJECT OF THE GAME: Free your group's king or queen and bring them safely over the center line.

GO!

DIRECTIONS: This game is best played outdoors or in a gymnasium. Lay the *jump-ropes* down the center of the playing area. Place each *bandanna* 20 feet behind the center line on each side. Designate one side of the center line as a jail. Have kids form two groups and stand on opposite sides of the center line. Let each group choose a King or Queen to be a prisoner and stand on the opponent's *bandanna*. Then have each group choose a Guard to guard the opponents' "royalty." The rest of the players may run anywhere on their side of the center line.

> **INSIDE TIP**
> Older kids love this fast-paced rescue game! Let the winning team line up first for much-needed drinks of water after playing.

Say: **This is a royal rescue game! Your group will attempt to rescue your King or Queen without getting tagged by the Guard or your opponents. If you're tagged, go to jail until one of your team members runs to tag you free. Then the two of you may safely return to your side and resume playing. If you reach the King or Queen without being tagged, you've won the game.**

JAIL

MALL-BRAWL

GET READY...

GROUP SIZE: Any
BEST FOR GRADES: K-4
PLAYING TIME: 10 minutes
ENERGY LEVEL: High
ITEMS NEEDED: A *bandanna* and 1 less playing item than there are kids

GET SET...

OBJECT OF THE GAME: Rush to exchange purchases with someone else—but don't get caught without a package!

GO!

DIRECTIONS: Designate the "store" by placing a *bandanna* on the floor in the center of the playing area. Lay the playing items beside the store. Choose one player to be the Mall-Caller and then invite everyone else to choose a playing item from the store. Direct kids to spread out around the playing area.

> **INSIDE TIP**
>
> Try this game with older kids, too. They love the idea of malls, and the game is a great icebreaker when they exchange packages (and names!) with each other.

Say: **Everyone rushes to shop and exchange items in a mall. In this game you'll rush to exchange the item you have with the item someone else has. When the Mall-Caller says "mall-brawl," quickly rush to set your items in the center. Then choose a different item and return to your place. The Mall-Caller will also rush to pick up an item. The person left without a "package" becomes the next Mall-Caller. You must pick up a different item each time.**

FOLLOW-THE-LEADER TOSSUP

GET READY...

GROUP SIZE: Any
BEST FOR GRADES: K-3
PLAYING TIME: 10 minutes
ENERGY LEVEL: Medium
ITEMS NEEDED: The *playground ball* and 1 item for each player

GET SET...

OBJECT OF THE GAME: Follow the leader's tricks and then challenge the others with your tricks.

GO!

DIRECTIONS: Choose one player to be the Leader and give him or her the *playground ball*. Invite the rest of the players to each choose a playing item. Form a circle with the Leader in the center.

Say: **The Leader will toss the ball in the air and then do a trick such as clapping three times or twirling around before catching the ball. If the Leader makes a successful catch, imitate his or her trick using your item. If the Leader drops the ball, we'll choose another Leader. After the Leader does three tricks, we'll pass our items five places to the right and then choose a new Leader. Let's play until everyone has a chance to lead.**

Encourage the Leaders to devise new, unique tricks. When a new Leader steps to the center, have the player hand his or her item to the outgoing Leader.

BEE-BOP 'N' DOO-WOP

GET READY...

GROUP SIZE: Any
BEST FOR GRADES: 1-6
PLAYING TIME: 10 minutes
ENERGY LEVEL: Medium
ITEMS NEEDED: The *balloons*

GET SET...

OBJECT OF THE GAME: Have fun boppin' your *balloons* but be ready to switch directions in a wink.

GO!

DIRECTIONS: Hand each player a *balloon* to blow up and tie off. Help younger kids blow up and tie off their *balloons*. Stand in a close-knit circle.

Sing in your own little tune: **"Bee-bop 'n' doo-wop. Bee-bee-bop 'n' doo-wop."** '50s' songs are fun, and so is this

iNSiDE TiP

Try a different variation of this game. Bop one less *balloon* than there are kids around the circle. When you say "stop," the player without a *balloon* becomes the next "bee-bop 'n' doo-wop" caller.

game of *balloon* bee-bop. We'll start by bopping our *balloons* up and down. Then when I say "bee-bop," bop your *balloon* to the player on your right. Keep bopping to the right until I say "doo-wop," then reverse directions and bop your *balloon* to the player on your left. Keep bopping to the left and right depending on the call. When I finally say "stop," we'll see if you have a *balloon* to hold.

ALPHA-PASS

GET READY...

GROUP SIZE: Any
BEST FOR GRADES: K-6
PLAYING TIME: 15 minutes
ENERGY LEVEL: Low
ITEMS NEEDED: The *foam ball* and the *kitchen timer*

GET SET...

OBJECT OF THE GAME: Pass your way through the alphabet before time runs out.

GO!

DIRECTIONS: Form a circle. Hand one player the *foam ball*.

Say: **This is a game of fast catching and quick thinking. I'll name a category such as "food" and then begin the timer. I'll name a food that begins with the letter "a" such as artichoke. Then I'll quickly toss the ball to someone across the circle who will name a food beginning with the letter "b." If someone tosses you the ball and you've already named a food, toss the ball quickly to someone who hasn't had a turn. After everyone's participated, we'll repeat turns. Let's see if we can make it through the alphabet before time runs out.**

Play again using a category suggested below or make up more of your own. If you're playing with young children, omit the timer and let them simply repeat the alphabet letter by letter.

Categories may be
- animals,
- cereal names,
- names of girls or boys,
- names of states,
- objects in a classroom, or
- articles of clothing.

STASH-AND-DASH PiRATES

GET SET...

OBJECT OF THE GAME: Find all the hidden objects before time runs out.

Go!

DIRECTIONS: Choose two kids to be Pirates and hand them the *disks* and the *cups*. The rest of the children will be Dashers.

Say: **Pirates always stash their loot. In a moment the Dashers will hide their eyes and count to 20 while the Pirates hide their loot around the playing area. Then the Pirates will call out, "Stash and dash!" I'll begin the timer, and the Dashers can run to find the hidden loot and bring it back to the timer. We'll play until the loot is found or time runs out.**

Have the Dashers turn their backs to the Pirates as they count to 20. Continue playing until each player has been a Pirate and has had a chance to hide the loot.

GET READY...

GROUP SIZE: Any
BEST FOR GRADES: K-3
PLAYING TIME: 15 minutes
ENERGY LEVEL: Medium
ITEMS NEEDED: The *kitchen timer*, 6 *disks*, and 6 *cups*

iNSiDE TiP

The Pirates can give clues to help the Dashers, if they're having trouble finding the loot. Have Pirates clap more quickly, the closer the Dashers get to finding the hidden loot.

ACCELER-ATE!

GET READY...

GROUP SIZE: 5 or more
BEST FOR GRADES: 1-4
PLAYING TIME: 10 minutes
ENERGY LEVEL: Low
ITEMS NEEDED: The *playground ball*

GET SET...

OBJECT OF THE GAME: Toss the ball faster and faster in a fixed pattern without dropping it.

GO!

DIRECTIONS: Have everyone stand in a circle. If you have more than eight kids, form two or three smaller circles. Hand one player the *playground ball*.

> **INSIDE TIP**
>
> If you have a very large group, make a smaller circle and use any toss-able playing item such as the *color* or *number cubes* or the *cups*.

Say: **Let's have some fun making patterns. The first person will toss the ball to someone in the circle. Then that player will toss the ball to someone else and so on. Each person should throw the ball to someone new until everyone in the circle has caught the ball once. Then we'll begin the pattern all over again. Remember who you tossed the ball to! Keep tossing in your pattern until I say "Accelerate!" Then speed up your tossing until I say "Brakes!" or someone drops the ball. Then we'll stop and begin a new pattern.**

Wait until the kids are familiar with the tossing pattern before calling out "Accelerate!" After a few rounds, try adding a second ball for really exciting play!

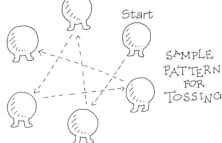

SAMPLE PATTERN FOR TOSSING

ACROSS THE BORDER

GET READY...

GROUP SIZE: 9 or more
BEST FOR GRADES: 3-6
PLAYING TIME: 15 minutes
ENERGY LEVEL: High
ITEMS NEEDED: The *masking tape*, *6 cups*, and the *kitchen timer*

GET SET...

OBJECT OF THE GAME: Have the least number of *cups* behind your goal line when time runs out.

GO!

DIRECTIONS: Place three 4-foot *masking tape* lines on the playing field. Place the lines opposite each other about 15 feet apart. Form three groups and have each group choose a "Goalie." (If there are more than nine children in each group, have each group choose two Goalies.) Direct each Goalie to stand in front of a *masking tape* line. Set the six *cups* in the center. Tell the rest of the kids to stand near the *cups*.

Say: **In this game you'll try to get *cups* over the other groups' goal lines. When I start the timer and say "go," grab a *cup* and attempt to set it behind any opponent's goal line. The Goalie's job is to quickly return the *cups* to the center. You may only carry one *cup* at a time. We'll play until time runs out and I say "freeze." Then we'll count the *cups* behind each goal line.**

Begin the game and play until time runs out. If you're using two Goalies for each group, have the winning team cut back to one Goalie for the next round.

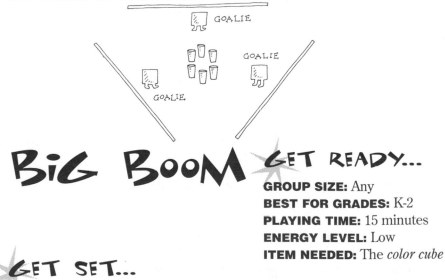

BiG BOOM

GET READY...

GROUP SIZE: Any
BEST FOR GRADES: K-2
PLAYING TIME: 15 minutes
ENERGY LEVEL: Low
ITEM NEEDED: The *color cube*

GET SET...

OBJECT OF THE GAME: Don't be caught with the TNT in this exciting counting game.

Go!

DIRECTIONS: Form a circle. Choose a player to be "It." Have It choose a number between one and 25 and whisper it to you. This number is the Big Boom.

Say: **This is an exciting game of counting. It chose a number between one and 25 and whispered that number to** me. **We'll begin passing the** *color cube* **around the circle. As we pass it, we'll count, "One, two, three, four, five" and so on until we get to the number that's the Big Boom. Then It will shout, "Big Boom!" and the player holding the** *color cube* **comes to the center and becomes It.**

iNSiDE TiP

If your group is very large, pass two items and choose two Big-Boom numbers.

Continue playing until each player has been It. You may want to play the game like Musical Chairs and have the kids sit in the center of the circle after they've received a Big Boom. Play until one child remains in the circle. Older kids may enjoy using higher numbers that are multiples of five or 10, then counting by fives or tens to reach that number.

PUT OUT THE FiRE

GET READY...

GROUP SIZE: Any
BEST FOR GRADES: K-6
PLAYING TIME: 15 minutes
ENERGY LEVEL: High
ITEMS NEEDED: 6 *cups* and water

GET SET...

OBJECT OF THE GAME: Cool off with exciting water fun.

Go!

DIRECTIONS: This game is best played outdoors on a hot summer day. Be sure kids are in swimsuits or clothes that can get wet. Fill six *cups* with water and place them around the playing field. Gather the kids at one end of the playing field.

Say: **It's a hot day, and you look like sizzling matches that need cooling off with a bit of water. When I say, "Put out the fire!" run to a *cup* and stick one of your fingers in the water. You may have up to four people at each *cup*. The** next time I say, "Put out the fire," run to a different *cup* and stick two fingers in the water. If a *cup* tips over, the people at that *cup* must sit down for the remainder of the game. We'll play until we get to 10 fingers or until all the *cups* are tipped over.

Refill the *cups* after the first round and let kids play once more. Be sure to invite kids to have cool drinks of water in paper *cups* when you're finished playing!

POWER-PARTNER POLO

GET READY...

GROUP SIZE: 8 or more
BEST FOR GRADES: 2-6
PLAYING TIME: 15 minutes
ENERGY LEVEL: High
ITEMS NEEDED: 2 *jump-ropes* and 6 *cups*

GET SET...

OBJECT OF THE GAME: Kick the *cup* across your opponent's goal line.

GO!

DIRECTIONS: This game needs a large playing area and is best suited for outside or gymnasium play. Lay the *jump-ropes* 50 feet apart as goal lines and set six *cups* in the center of the playing area. Have kids form two groups and stand on opposite sides of the *cups*. Instruct kids to find partners and lock arms.

Say: **In this game of polo, partners will run and kick *cups* over their opponents' goal line. Keep your arms locked—no hands are allowed in this game. You may block your opponents' shots to prevent them from kicking *cups* over your group's goal line. And you may "steal" the *cup* by kicking it away from your opponents. When a *cup* goes over a goal line, leave it there until the end of the game. We'll play until all the *cups* are over the goal lines.**

When all the *cups* are over the goal lines, count the number of *cups* on each side. The group with the fewest number may choose the next game.

BACKPACK PASS

⭐ GET READY...

GROUP SIZE: Any
BEST FOR GRADES: 1-6
PLAYING TIME: 10 minutes
ENERGY LEVEL: Medium
ITEMS NEEDED: The *color* and *number cubes*

⭐ GET SET...

OBJECT OF THE GAME: Wiggle and jiggle to pass the backpack down your line.

⭐ GO!

DIRECTIONS: Form two groups and instruct each group to line up on their hands and knees.

Say: **I can see you're on pretend school buses ready for school. But you forgot your backpacks!** Place a cube on the back of the first person in each line. **When I say "go," pass your "backpack" to the end of your bus. You'll have to wiggle and jiggle to pass it —no hands allowed! If the backpack falls off a player, that player goes to the back of the bus. Then the next person in line sets the backpack on his or her back and passes it on. The first group** to pass the backpack to the end of the bus wins.

INSIDE TIP

Let kids pass the backpack in different ways, such as with their feet, their knees, or their elbows.

LOST SHEEP

GET READY...

GROUP SIZE: Any
BEST FOR GRADES: K-3
PLAYING TIME: 15 minutes
ENERGY LEVEL: Low
ITEMS NEEDED: The *kitchen timer*, *2 bandannas*, and the *number* and *color cube*s

GET SET...

OBJECT OF THE GAME: Find the lost sheep before time runs out.

GO!

DIRECTIONS: Have kids form a circle sitting on the floor. Choose two kids to be "Shepherds" and blindfold them.

Say: **Our two Shepherds have lost a "sheep" and must crawl on their hands and knees to find it. The timer will be our pretend sheep**. Wind up the timer and set it somewhere in the circle. **If you're very quiet, you can hear the lost sheep.** Listen for the tick of the timer. Then say: **All right, Shepherds, go find your lost sheep.**

Play until one of the Shepherds has found the sheep. Then blindfold two more children and hide the timer. Play until each child has been a Shepherd.

INSIDE TIP

For a fun variation or if you're using a timer that doesn't make ticking sounds, choose only one Shepherd. Hide the *color cube* and let the kids in the circle clap faster as the Shepherd moves closer to the sheep and slower when he or she moves away.

RAHAB RAG TAG

GET READY...

GROUP SIZE: Any
BEST FOR GRADES: K-6
PLAYING TIME: 15 minutes
ENERGY LEVEL: High
ITEMS NEEDED: *2 bandannas*

GET SET...

OBJECT OF THE GAME: Grab Rahab's rope before you're tagged out.

GO!

DIRECTIONS: This is a great game to reinforce your study of Joshua at Jericho. Gather kids in the center of the playing area. Choose two children whose birthdays are closest to today's date to be "Rahabs." Hand the Rahabs the *bandannas* and tell them to place the *bandannas* on their shoulders or heads.

Say: **Let's pretend the *bandannas* in this game are Rahab's red rope. When I say, "Rahab rag-tag," try to snatch the "rope" from each Rahab without getting tagged. If either Rahab tags you, you must sit out for the remainder of the round. Whoever snatches a rope becomes Rahab in the next game.**

> **INSIDE TIP**
> This game can easily be adapted for inside play. Clear a space in the classroom and instruct kids to walk heel to toe or backward to play.

Continue playing until each child has been Rahab. Add an extra challenge for older players by choosing a partner to guard each Rahab from the rope snatchers. The guards may tag players, instead of Rahab.

GUARDIAN ANGELS

GET READY...

GROUP SIZE: Any
BEST FOR GRADES: K-6
PLAYING TIME: 15 minutes
ENERGY LEVEL: High
ITEMS NEEDED: 6 *cups* and the *playground ball*

GET SET...

OBJECT OF THE GAME: Pretend to be angels and guard Daniel from the lion's jaws.

GO!

DIRECTIONS: Hand a *cup* to each player and tell kids these are "Daniels." If you have more than six players, let kids play in pairs. (For really large groups, omit the *cups* and play with threesomes: two guardian angels and one child as Daniel.) Instruct the players to set their *cups* on the floor and stand beside them.

Say: **In this game you're all guardian angels, and you're guarding Daniel, your *cup*, from the jaws of a ferocious** lion! Hold up the *playground ball*. **This ball is our pretend lion. You'll roll the lion at each other's Daniel and try to knock it over. Guard Daniel by deflecting the lion with your feet. No hands are allowed in this game, so you'll have to roll—not kick—the ball with your feet! We'll play until there's only one Daniel left standing.**

iNSiDE TiP

Older kids love this game as much as younger players! For a twist, have kids form a circle and place the *cups* inside the circle. Choose two or three "guardian angels" and let kids in the circle roll the lion quickly back and forth across the circle as the angels guard the *cups* from tipping over.

STEP ACROSS THE SEA

GET READY...

GROUP SIZE: Any
BEST FOR GRADES: K-2
PLAYING TIME: 10 minutes
ENERGY LEVEL: Medium
ITEMS NEEDED: 6 *disks* and 2 *bandannas*

GET SET...

OBJECT OF THE GAME: Don't fall in the sea as you step across the stones.

GO!

DIRECTIONS: Lay the *bandannas* at opposite ends of the classroom or 20 feet apart in a larger play area. Place the *disks* at equal intervals between the *bandannas*. Gather kids behind one of the *bandannas*.

Say: **What a big sea we must cross! And we can only step on the *disks* or "stones" to cross it. We'll start at the *bandanna* and hop from stone to stone until we reach the other *bandanna*. Each time we cross the sea without falling in, we'll spread the stones a little farther apart. Do you think we can cross the sea three or four or even five times?**

Each time everyone makes it across the sea, move the *disks* a few more inches apart. You may even have to remove a *disk* if your class is full of leaps and bounds!

BALLOON SERENADE

GET READY...

GROUP SIZE: Any
BEST FOR GRADES: 3-6
PLAYING TIME: 10 minutes
ENERGY LEVEL: Low
ITEMS NEEDED: The *balloons* and a *ruler*

GET SET...

OBJECT OF THE GAME: Outlast the entire orchestra with your *balloon* serenade.

GO!

DIRECTIONS: This game is great fun but best played in an outside "amphitheater" where others won't be disturbed by the serenades! Hand each player a *balloon*. Instruct kids to blow up the *balloons* and hold the ends to prevent escaping air.

Say: **You're part of the Squeak 'n Squawk *Balloon* Orchestra. I'll be your conductor.** Swing the *ruler* a few times back and forth like a conductor's baton. **When I say "begin," create your own serenade by letting squeaky sounds come from your *balloon*. Watch my baton as I conduct the orchestra! When I wave the baton faster, play faster. But if I slow down, you slow down, too. We'll play until the very last squeaky-squawking note. Whoever plays the last note of the serenade becomes the next conductor.**

At the end of the serenade, hand the *ruler* to the next conductor and have kids blow up their *balloons* for the second overture. End your serenade with a bang by having kids blow up their *balloons*, tie them, then sit on the *balloons* on the count of three.

FUNNY FISHING

GET READY...

GROUP SIZE: Any
BEST FOR GRADES: 2-6
PLAYING TIME: 15 minutes
ENERGY LEVEL: Low
ITEMS NEEDED: The *masking tape*, 2 *jump-ropes*, 2 *Ping-Pong balls*, 6 *disks*, 6 *cups*, and 2 *bandannas*

GET SET...

OBJECT OF THE GAME: Be the first group of Fishers to pull in your catch.

GO!

DIRECTIONS: Invite kids to form two groups of "Fishers" and hand each group a *jump-rope* "fishing pole." Let groups each choose a "Fish," and have Fish stand three feet from their groups. Place a *Ping-Pong ball*, a *bandanna*, three *cups*, and three *disks* beside each Fish. Set the *masking tape* between the Fish.

Say: **It's a fine day to go fishing! The first Fisher in each group will cast a line** *(jump-rope)* **to the Fish. The Fish must tear off a piece of** *masking tape* **and tape an item on the end of the line. Tug on the line, and the Fisher can pull in the catch. Then the Fisher runs to become the next Fish, and the Fish runs to join the group of Fishers. We'll continue until all your items have been caught and reeled in!**

If your group is large, have two players be Fish and let the Fishers take turns casting the lines.

GALLOPING GOLIATHS

GET READY..

GROUP SIZE: Any
BEST FOR GRADES: 4-6
PLAYING TIME: 10 minutes
ENERGY LEVEL: High
ITEMS NEEDED: 2 *jump-ropes*, 2 *bandannas*, and 6 *cups*

GET SET...

OBJECT OF THE GAME: Be the first group of galloping Goliaths through the obstacle course.

Go!

DIRECTIONS: Place the *jump-ropes* at one end of the playing area and the *bandannas* at the opposite end to create two start and finish lines. Stagger the *cups* between the start and finish lines making sure there are at least three feet between each *cup*. Instruct kids to form threesomes. Have the trios line up behind the starting lines.

> **INSIDE TIP**
>
> Older kids may enjoy another mode of travel! Have two people get on their hands and knees and the third player can "ride" on their backs to the finish line. Switch places for the return trip.

Say: **The Bible tells us that Goliath was giant-sized. Maybe even as big as three kids! Your threesomes are "Goliaths" in this race. When I say "go," two players in each trio will cross arms and grasp each other's wrists. The third person will sit on their arms. Walk and weave around the three** *cups* **until you reach the finish line. Then your trio can grab hands and run back to the starting line. When all the Goliaths in your group have finished, sit down and shout "Go-li-ath!"**

START

ONE, TWO, STUCK LIKE GLUE!

GET READY...

GROUP SIZE: Any
BEST FOR GRADES: K-6
PLAYING TIME: 15 minutes
ENERGY LEVEL: High
ITEM NEEDED: A *bandanna*

GET SET...

OBJECT OF THE GAME: Take two giant steps but don't get tagged with the *bandanna*.

Go!

DIRECTIONS: Have kids stand in a circle and number off around the circle. Choose the person who's birthday is closest to Christmas to be the Tosser and have that person stand in the center holding the *bandanna*.

Say: **One, two, this game's for you. One, two, here's what you do! The Tosser will toss the** *bandanna* **high in the air and call out a number between one and** (player with the highest number). **The player with that number will run to grab the** *bandanna* **while the rest of us take two giant steps away from the center. After two steps, you're stuck like glue to that spot! Then the Tosser takes two giant steps to get close enough to toss the** *bandanna* **and tag someone with it. The tagged person becomes the next Tosser. If the Tosser doesn't tag anyone, he or she remains the Tosser for the next turn.**

Play until everyone has been the Tosser at least once.

RAD RELAY

GET READY...

GROUP SIZE: Any
BEST FOR GRADES: 2-6
PLAYING TIME: 15 minutes
ENERGY LEVEL: Medium
ITEMS NEEDED: The *number cube*, the *kitchen timer*, and the *balloons*

GET SET...

OBJECT OF THE GAME: Keep up the passing frenzy as you add more and more *balloons*.

Go!

DIRECTIONS: Blow up and tie off as many *balloons* as there are players. Have kids form a circle on the floor and let them each roll the *number cube*. Tell them to remember whether their numbers are "even" or "odd." Then set the *number cube* aside.

Say: **In this wild passing game, the way you pass** *balloons* **depends on whether you're an even or odd number.** "Evens" **will pass** *balloons* **with their feet;** "Odds" **will**

> ### iNSiDE TiP
> Young children might enjoy playing with only a few *balloons* and without the extra challenge of a timer.

pass *balloons* with their elbows. I'll start the timer, then we'll begin passing one *balloon*. I'll add more, so be ready! We'll see if we can have all the *balloons* in play before time runs out.

After the first round, vary the way Evens and Odds pass *balloons*. Use the following suggestions or let kids devise their own. Pass

- with pinkie fingers,
- under knees,
- behind backs,
- with palms of hands,
- on fingertips,
- over your heads,
- laying down, or
- with your eyes closed.

HOT POTATO TAG

GET READY...

GROUP SIZE: 12 or more
BEST FOR GRADES: 2-6
PLAYING TIME: 15 minutes
ENERGY LEVEL: High
ITEM NEEDED: A *disk*

GET SET...

OBJECT OF THE GAME: Don't get caught holding the Hot Potato in this wild game of chase.

GO!

DIRECTIONS: Direct kids to form two rows of passengers as in an airplane with an aisle down the middle (see diagram). Choose one child to be the Hot Potato and hand him or her the *disk*. Choose another child to be the Tagger. Have the Hot Potato and the Tagger stand on opposite sides of the rows.

Say: **This is a great game of chasing and changing seats. You're on an "airplane," and the Tagger wants to tag the Hot Potato. They'll run around and around the seats. The Hot Potato can hand the *disk* to another player and sit in his or her seat any time. Then that player must jump up and run from the Tagger before being caught. If the Tagger** catches you, you're the next Tagger and the Tagger becomes the Hot Potato.

If your group is very large, you may wish to play with three rows of passengers and use two *disks* for Hot Potatoes.

MOUSE IN THE HOUSE

GET READY...

GROUP SIZE: Any
BEST FOR GRADES: K-2
PLAYING TIME: 15 minutes
ENERGY LEVEL: Medium
ITEMS NEEDED: The *color cube* and a *bandanna*

GET SET...

OBJECT OF THE GAME: Pretend to be a hungry mouse and find your cheese.

GO!

DIRECTIONS: Choose one player to be the "mouse" and blindfold him or her using the *bandanna*. Assign the rest of the kids a room of the house such as a bedroom, living room, attic, bathroom, basement, or kitchen. Be sure no two kids have the same room. Instruct them to stand in the center of the play area with their feet spread apart so the mouse can crawl through the "mouse holes." Set the *color-cube* "cheese" in one room of the house between that player's feet.

Say: **I see a hungry mouse. But there's a yummy piece of cheese in the** (name of the room). **The**

INSIDE TIP

For another variation, have kids scatter and sit on the floor. "Hide" the cube on the floor and let the mouse crawl to find it as players give clues by squeaking in tiny voices when the mouse is far away and squeaking loudly as the mouse gets closer to the cheese.

mouse must crawl through the house to find it. If the mouse touches you, tell the mouse what room he is in. The mouse can keep crawling until it reaches the (name of the room) **and finds the cheese.**

Continue playing until each player has been the mouse.

BOOMER-ANG!

GET READY...

GROUP SIZE: 10 or more
BEST FOR GRADES: K-6
PLAYING TIME: 15 minutes
ENERGY LEVEL: High
ITEMS NEEDED: 6 *disks* and 6 *cups*

GET SET...

OBJECT OF THE GAME: Be the last person "free" in this zany game of Tag.

GO!

DIRECTIONS: Spread the *disks* and *cups* around the playing area as bases. You'll only need one *disk* or one *cup* for each player. (If your group is very large, have kids pair up.) Direct each player to stand by a base.

Say: **In this game you'll try to tag others out while you're running to a safe base. When I say "boomerang," run to stand at another safe base. If you're touching a *disk* right now, you'll run to touch a *cup*. And if you're touching a *cup*, you'll run to find a *disk*. As you're running, you may tag others out—but don't get tagged yourself! Then when I say "boomerang" again, run to find another base. If you're tagged, you must sit out for the rest of the game. We'll keep switching bases until there's only one person who hasn't been tagged.**

When there's only one player left untagged, have that person choose the next game or line up first for drinks.

UFO

✦ GET READY...

GROUP SIZE: Any
BEST FOR GRADES: 3-6
PLAYING TIME: 15 minutes
ENERGY LEVEL: Medium
ITEMS NEEDED: 2 *jump-ropes*,
3 *disks*, and the *kitchen timer*

✦ GET SET...

OBJECT OF THE GAME: Don't get captured by the aliens!

✦ GO!

DIRECTIONS: This game is best played outdoors or in a gymnasium. Tie the *jump-ropes* together and lay them in a circle at one side of the playing field as the capture area. Choose three kids to be Space Commanders and hand each a "UFO" disk. (If your group is very large, use six *disks*.)

Say: **The flying saucers have landed and the Commanders are looking for you! I'll start the timer. The Space Commanders will toss their flying saucer *disks* like Frisbees. If you're tagged by a flying *disk*, you must go to the capture area. If a friend sneaks over and grabs your hand, you're free to play again. See if you can keep from being tagged until time runs out. Then we'll choose three new Space Commanders.**

Young children love this game of keep away from the aliens. Add an extra challenge for older kids by placing six *cups* around the playing area. Tell the kids they're to snatch the *cups* without being tagged by a flying saucer.

TRIM THE TREE

✦ GET READY...

GROUP SIZE: 6 or more
BEST FOR GRADES: K-3
PLAYING TIME: 15 minutes
ENERGY LEVEL: Medium
ITEMS NEEDED: 2 *bandannas*, the
color and *number cubes*, 2 *jump-ropes*, and 6 *disks*

GET SET...

OBJECT OF THE GAME: Be the first group of "elves" to decorate your human Christmas tree.

GO!

DIRECTIONS: Have a little fun with Christmas in July—or any month! Form two groups of "elves" and give each group the following "ornaments": a *bandanna*, a cube, a *jump-rope*, and three *disks*. Let groups decide which players will be human Christmas trees first.

Say: **What a speedy group of elves I see. And such tall Christmas trees! When I say, "Merry Christmas," the elves will decorate the Christmas trees with their decorations. The last ornament on your tree should be the cube. Be sure to place the cube at the top of your Christmas tree. When your tree is all decorated, begin singing "Jingle Bells." We'll see which group of elves are the quickest tree decorators.**

Play until each elf has been the Christmas tree. You may wish to vary the song kids sing when their trees are decorated. Consider ending your game time by serving candy canes or Christmas cookies for a winning treat.

LETTER-GETTER

GET READY...

GROUP SIZE: 8 or more
BEST FOR GRADES: 1-3
PLAYING TIME: 15 minutes
ENERGY LEVEL: Low
ITEMS NEEDED: 2 *jump-ropes*

GET SET...

OBJECT OF THE GAME: Help your group form letters of the alphabet.

GO!

DIRECTIONS: Tell kids to form two groups and hand each group a *jump-rope*.

Say: **You all know your alphabet very well. You've probably written each letter with crayons, markers, pencils, and** pens lots of times. But have you ever written letters with a rope? I'll call out a letter of the alphabet. See how quickly you can make that letter with your *jump-rope* and then sit down. If your group finishes first, each group member must name a word that begins with that letter.

Continue playing until you've worked your way through the entire alphabet. As an extra challenge, have kids use their bodies to form letters. Or try naming words that fit into a specific category such as foods, kids' names, or animals.

JOLLY BALL

GET READY...

GROUP SIZE: 8 or more
BEST FOR GRADES: 2-6
PLAYING TIME: 15 minutes
ENERGY LEVEL: High
ITEMS NEEDED: 2 *jump-ropes* and the *foam ball*

GET SET...

OBJECT OF THE GAME: Play a cooperative game of volleyball and get the giggles.

GO!

DIRECTIONS: Establish a center line by laying the *jump-ropes* end to end down the middle of the playing area. Have kids form two groups and number off by threes in their groups. Tell the ones that they'll be the "Ha's," the twos they'll be the "Hee's," and the threes they'll be the "Ho's."

Say: **Volleyball is a fun game, but Jolly Ball is even more fun! In this game, you must volley the ball three times before it goes over the *jump-rope* "net." First, #1 must volley the ball to #2 in your group and say "ha!" Then #2 says "hee!" as he or she volleys the ball to #3. Then #3 says "ho!" and volleys the ball over the net to your opponents. We'll see how quickly you can keep volleying. Every time you get the ball over the net, you'll score 1 point. We'll play until one side has 5 points.**

After each game, have groups switch sides of the net. Play until one group has won two games, then let that group line up first for drinks.

TRiANGLE DODGE BALL

GET READY...

GROUP SIZE: 9 or more
BEST FOR GRADES: K-6
PLAYING TIME: 15 minutes
ENERGY LEVEL: High
ITEMS NEEDED: The *masking tape* and the *playground ball*

GET SET...

OBJECT OF THE GAME: Keep from getting tagged out in this crazy three-way game.

GO!

DIRECTIONS: Mark off three sides of a triangle with 6-foot lengths of *masking tape*. Extend the sides out a few feet for additional "dodge space" (see diagram). Have kids form three groups and stand behind each of the three *masking tape* lines. Explain that these are goal lines and players must stay behind the lines or they're out. Designate the inside triangle as the Free Zone where no players may stand.

Say: **I'll bounce the ball in the Free Zone to begin the game. You may toss the ball at waist level or below to try and tag someone in another group. If you're tagged, you must join that group. If you catch the ball when some-**

>
> **iNSiDE TiP**
>
> If your group is very large, make a *masking tape* square on the floor and play four-way dodge ball. Play until there are only two groups left.

one else tosses it, the person who threw the ball must join your group. We'll play until one group is left.

For extra dodge-ball frenzy, play with more than one ball.

SEESAW TAG

GET READY...

GROUP SIZE: Any
BEST FOR GRADES: K-4
PLAYING TIME: 10 minutes
ENERGY LEVEL: High
ITEMS NEEDED: 2 *bandannas*

GET SET...

OBJECT OF THE GAME: Join with your group to create a see-saw and then hop up and down as you try to snatch your opponents' flag.

Go!

DIRECTIONS: Direct kids to count off by twos and send groups to opposite sides of the playing area. Hand each group a *bandanna* and let them decide who will be the Flag Carriers. Have the Flag Carriers tuck the *bandannas* in their belts or waistbands. (If they're not wearing belts or don't have waistbands, the Flag Carriers may hold the *bandannas* in their hands.)

Say: **This game will get us hopping! When I say "scatter," run around the playing area. When I say "stop," freeze in place. The Flag Carriers will hop to someone in their group and take that person's hand. Then the two players will hop to another group member and take his or her hand. When you've made a seesaw by collecting all your group members, hop to your opponents and try to snatch their flag. The first seesaw that gets the flag wins.**

If you play again, renumber kids so they have a chance to be with different people.

NOAH'S RAINBOW CATCH

GET READY...

GROUP SIZE: Any
BEST FOR GRADES: K-2
PLAYING TIME: 15 minutes
ENERGY LEVEL: High
ITEMS NEEDED: 2 *jump-ropes*, a *bandanna*, and the *color cube*

GET SET...

OBJECT OF THE GAME: Make it to the rainbow without being tagged by Noah.

GO!

DIRECTIONS: Tie one end of one *jump-rope* to the other. Lay the *jump-ropes* at one end of the playing area in an arch shape. Tell kids this is the rainbow. Place the *bandanna* off to one side of the playing area and designate it as the "paint pot." Gather kids at the opposite end of the playing area. Assign each player a color (red, yellow, green, or blue) and tell kids to remember their colors. Choose the child whose birthday is closest to today's date to be "Noah" and hand him or her the *color cube*.

Say: **Rainbows are beautiful, and we're going to make a pretend rainbow in our game. Noah will roll the *color cube***

> **INSIDE TIP**
> A different twist might be to let players who are tagged become Noahs and help tag others.

and tell the color. All players with that color may walk heel to toe to the rainbow. Noah may also walk heel to toe to tag you. If Noah touches you, you must go to the paint pot, or *bandanna*. If you make it safely to the rainbow, stand on the rainbow until all the colors are in place. We'll see if at least one of every color makes it to the rainbow.

Play until all the kids are either in the paint pot or standing on the rainbow. Then choose another child to be Noah. You may wish to let kids run, skip, hop, or walk backward to the rainbow. Be sure Noah moves in the same way to tag players. Play until each child has been Noah.

ROLLER RACERS

GET READY...

GROUP SIZE: 9 or more
BEST FOR GRADES: 1-6
PLAYING TIME: 15 minutes
ENERGY LEVEL: Medium
ITEMS NEEDED: The *color* and *number cubes* and the *masking tape*

GET SET...

OBJECT OF THE GAME: Switch places in this fast-paced race—but don't get caught without a seat.

Go!

DIRECTIONS: Hand one player the *color* and *number cubes*. Give the rest of the players each a 5-inch piece of *masking tape*. Have kids spread out around the playing area and stick their tape to the floor. Direct kids to sit on their tape. Assign the players each a color (red, yellow, green, or blue) or a number from one to four.

> **iNSiDE TiP**
>
> This is a great rainy day game to work the wiggles out and keep kids on their toes.

Say: **This is a fast-switch game. The Roller will roll both the *color* and *number cubes* and tell the color and number rolled. The players with that color and number will leap up and rush to switch places. The Roller will try to find a vacant piece of tape, too. The player left without a piece of tape to sit on becomes the next Roller.**

Play until most kids have been the Roller.

ROW YOUR BOAT

GET READY...

GROUP SIZE: 6 or more
BEST FOR GRADES: 4-6
PLAYING TIME: 10 minutes
ENERGY LEVEL: Medium
ITEMS NEEDED: 2 *bandannas*, 6 *cups*, and the *rulers*

GET SET...

OBJECT OF THE GAME: Row your boat around the buoys and back to the dock.

Go!

DIRECTIONS: Place the *bandannas* at one end of the playing area as the "docks." Stagger the *cups* in a row down the playing area as "buoys." Be sure there are at least three feet between each *cup*. Have kids form two groups and think of names for their boats. Let each group choose a player to be the Rower and hand the Rower a *ruler* "oar." Tell groups to stand beside the docks.

Say: **Your boat is at the dock but in a moment, you'll head out to sea. When I say, "Row your boats," the boat members will grasp wrists and make a boat for the Rower to sit on. Then the boat and Rower will paddle in and out of the buoys. When you get to the last buoy, paddle back to the dock. If at any time I shout, "Lifeboat drill!" you must quickly stop and reorganize your boat with a new Rower to paddle. The first boat back to the dock wins.**

Begin the game. Be sure to call out, "Lifeboat drill!" a few times during the race. Have two or three races, then have the team with the most wins choose the next game or line up first to leave.

SECRET WORD

GET READY...

GROUP SIZE: Any
BEST FOR GRADES: K-4
PLAYING TIME: 15 minutes
ENERGY LEVEL: Low
ITEMS NEEDED: A *Ping-Pong ball*, a *bandanna*, the *foam ball*, a *disk*, a *jump-rope*, a *cube*, a *ruler*, a *cup*, and the *kitchen timer*

GET SET...

OBJECT OF THE GAME: Guess the secret item before time runs out.

GO!

DIRECTIONS: Set the *Ping-Pong ball*, the *bandanna*, the *disk*, the *jump-rope*, the *foam ball*, the *cube*, and the *cup* in a row. Place the timer off to one side. Help kids number off by threes and then sit in front of the items in their groups.

Say: **In this game you'll help your group figure out the secret item before time runs out. In a moment I'll have one group close their eyes while the other group secretly selects an item. That group will whisper the name of the item in my ear. Then we'll start the timer. You can ask questions to fig-** ure out the item such as **"Does it roll?" "Can it bounce?"** or **"Is it flat?" When you think you know what the secret item is, choose one person in your group to venture a guess. Be careful because you only have two chances to make a guess! See if you can figure out what the secret item is before time runs out.**

After one group has chosen a secret item, switch and let the other group choose. Play until one group has successfully guessed three times.

> ### INSIDE TIP
> For young children, try this twist. While one group hides their eyes, let the other group secretly snatch two of the items. Then have the other group guess which items are missing. Omit the timer for this version.

BALLOON SOCCER

GET READY...

GROUP SIZE: 8 or more
BEST FOR GRADES: 3-6
PLAYING TIME: 15 minutes
ENERGY LEVEL: High
ITEMS NEEDED: The *balloons* and 2 *bandannas*

GET SET...

OBJECT OF THE GAME: Prevent the other group from scoring by popping *balloons*.

GO!

DIRECTIONS: Blow up and tie off a *balloon* for each player. Place the *bandannas* at opposite ends of the playing area as goal lines. Have kids number off by twos and send groups to opposite sides of the playing area. Let each group choose a Goalie. Instruct the Goalies to stand beside the *bandanna* on the opposite side of the playing area from their group. Hand each group two *balloons*.

Say: **You'll really get a bang out of this soccer game! When I say "go," begin kicking the *balloons* toward your Goalie on the opposite side of the playing field. When the Goalie gets hold of a *balloon*, he or she must sit on the *balloon* and pop it. When a *balloon* pops, I'll toss another one into the game. You may steal your opponents' *balloons* and get them to your Goalie for extra points, but you can't use your hands. Only Goalies may use their hands in this game. We'll keep playing until all the *balloons* are popped. Then we'll count the popped *balloons* to see which group wins that round.**

Play two rounds or until your *balloons* are used up.

CATAPULT!

GET READY...

GROUP SIZE: Any
BEST FOR GRADES: 2-6
PLAYING TIME: 15 minutes
ENERGY LEVEL: Medium
ITEMS NEEDED: The *balloons*, 2 *bandannas*, a *disk*, and water

GET SET...

OBJECT OF THE GAME: Catapult your water *balloon* the farthest.

GO!

DIRECTIONS: This game is best played outdoors on a hot summer day. Be sure kids are wearing swimsuits or clothes that can get wet. Make a water *balloon* for each player. Have kids form two groups and give each group a *bandanna* and a water *balloon*. Tell the groups to decide who will be the "Catchers." The rest of the group members will be the "catapulters."

Say: **Let's cool off with a little fun. One group of catapulters will hold the *bandanna* around the edges and set the water *balloon* in the center. We'll count to three, then they'll catapult the water *balloon* into the air and as far out in the playing field as they can. The Catcher will run to catch the *balloon* as it comes down. If the Catcher catches the *balloon* without it popping, we'll mark the place it was caught with a *disk*. Then the next group will catapult their *balloon* and see if they can get it to go farther without popping. On the next catapult, we'll choose a new Catcher. We'll continue until everyone has been a Catcher.**

Be sure to pick up the *balloon* pieces at the end of the game.

SWiVEL-HOP

GET READY...

GROUP SIZE: Any
BEST FOR GRADES: K-4
PLAYING TIME: 15 minutes
ENERGY LEVEL: Medium
ITEMS NEEDED: The *playground ball* and the *kitchen timer*

GET SET...

OBJECT OF THE GAME: Swivel and hop but don't get caught! Be the last person in the lineup at the end of the game.

GO!

DIRECTIONS: Form two groups. Have one group stand in the center of the playing area. Have the other group count off by twos and line up on opposite sides of the center group (see diagram).

Say: **This is an unusual game of dodging the ball. The players in the center must only move in two directions: swiveling or hopping. And the moves must alternate. For example, the first time the ball is dodged, you may swivel by keeping one foot planted and swiveling around to avoid being tagged. The next time you dodge the ball you must hop. If you're tagged, join the other group. We'll play until time runs out and then switch places.**

Play until there are only one or two players left on a side. Then begin a new game but vary the two ways players can dodge the ball such as stooping or standing on one foot.

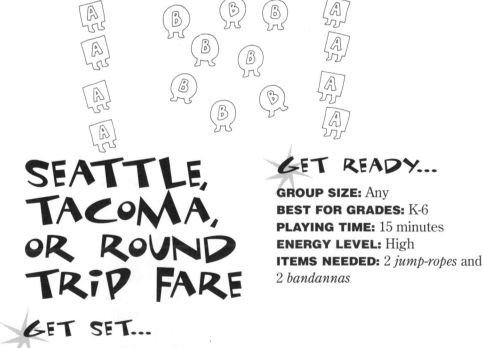

SEATTLE, TACOMA, OR ROUND TRIP FARE

GET READY...

GROUP SIZE: Any
BEST FOR GRADES: K-6
PLAYING TIME: 15 minutes
ENERGY LEVEL: High
ITEMS NEEDED: 2 *jump-ropes* and 2 *bandannas*

GET SET...

OBJECT OF THE GAME: Fly your airplane and land safely at the airport.

Go!

DIRECTIONS: Lay the *jump-ropes* in circles at opposite sides of the playing area. Designate one *jump-rope* as "Seattle" and the other as "Tacoma." Place the *bandannas* at opposite ends of the playing area as refueling airports. Choose one player to be the Air-Traffic Controller and have that person stand in the center. Instruct the rest of the players to stand beside either one of the *bandannas*.

Say: **You're airplanes at refueling airports. In a moment the Air-Traffic Controller will call out your flight plan—either Seattle, Tacoma, or refueling at another airport. Fly to that airport but don't get tagged along the way. If you're tagged, you become an Air-Traffic Controller and help tag other airplanes in flight. If the Controllers say, "Round trip," you must fly to each airport without getting tagged. You can't be tagged at an airport, but you can only stay at any one airport for a count of five before flying on. We'll play until there's only one airplane left flying.**

If you have a small group, remove one of the refueling airports. You may wish to form "jumbo jets" and let kids play in pairs.

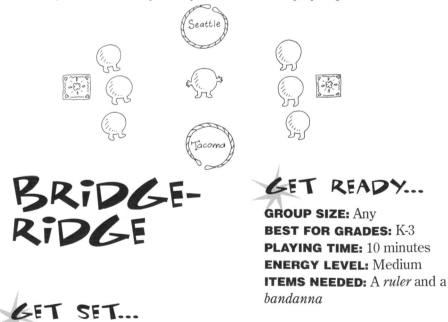

BRIDGE- RIDGE

GET READY...

GROUP SIZE: Any
BEST FOR GRADES: K-3
PLAYING TIME: 10 minutes
ENERGY LEVEL: Medium
ITEMS NEEDED: A *ruler* and a *bandanna*

GET SET...

OBJECT OF THE GAME: Work with the entire group to plant your flag on the moon.

Go!

DIRECTIONS: Tie the *bandanna* on one end of the *ruler* to make a flag. Gather kids at one end of the playing area and give the flag to a student.

Say: **Let's pretend we're the first kids on Mars, and we want to plant our flag to show we've been here. But, oh! There are lots of ridges and steep canyons to get over. The only way we'll get across Mars to plant our flag is by making a human bridge to get there! The first person will make a bridge by putting his or her hands on the floor and then the person with the flag will hand it to someone before crawling under the bridge. Then that person will add to the bridge. The player with the flag will hand it off before crawling under the bridge and so on. We'll continue handing off the flag and making the bridge until we've made it to the other side of Mars and can plant our flag.**

When you've crossed the playing area, set the flag down and encourage everyone to clap and cheer. Then return to your starting place using the human bridge.

JUGGLER-JiGGLE

GET READY...

GROUP SIZE: Up to 13
BEST FOR GRADES: 1-4
PLAYING TIME: 10 minutes
ENERGY LEVEL: Medium
ITEMS NEEDED: The *foam ball*, 6 *cups*, and 6 *disks*

GET SET...

OBJECT OF THE GAME: Juggle the items in and out—but don't drop a thing or *you'll* drop out!

Go!

DIRECTIONS: Let each person choose a playing item. Have kids form two groups facing each other two feet apart.

Say: **Not all jugglers are in the circus—we have jugglers here today! When I say "juggle," toss your item to someone in the other line. Catch an item and toss it to someone in the opposite line. If you drop an item, you must sit out. You may catch two or three items at once but toss them quickly to free up your hands. We'll play until there's only one juggler left.**

> **iNSiDE TiP**
>
> For variations on this juggling game, form different shapes such as a circle, triangle, or square. For an extra challenge with older players, juggle while sitting or kneeling.

KNoT AS EASY AS iT LooKS!

GET READY...

GROUP SIZE: 8 or more
BEST FOR GRADES: 3-6
PLAYING TIME: 15 minutes
ENERGY LEVEL: Medium
ITEM NEEDED: The *kitchen timer*

GET SET...

OBJECT OF THE GAME: Untangle yourselves and stop the timer before it runs out of time.

Go!

DIRECTIONS: Have kids hold hands and stretch out in a line across the playing area. Place the timer at one end of the line.

Say: **Knots in shoelaces are tough to untangle. In a moment you'll turn into a tangly knot, too! When I say "go," the players at each end of the line will begin going in and out and under and around to tie you up in knots. Don't let go of hands or the knot will break! Then I'll set the timer. We'll see if you can untangle yourselves without breaking the knot and grab the timer before it runs out.**

Older kids enjoy the challenge of untangling a human knot. Choose one player to turn his or her back while the group ties itself in a whopping knot. Then set the timer and have the player try to untangle the knot before time runs out.

SHOE DOMINOES

GET READY...

GROUP SIZE: Any
BEST FOR GRADES: K-6
PLAYING TIME: 15 minutes
ENERGY LEVEL: Low
ITEM NEEDED: The *kitchen timer*

GET SET...

OBJECT OF THE GAME: Find the matching shoes and place them side by side.

GO!

DIRECTIONS: Direct everyone to remove one shoe and place the shoes in a "bone pile." Scramble the bone pile and then let each player choose a shoe (that's not their own) to wear on their hands. Set the timer where everyone can see it.

Say: **Let's play an unusual game of dominoes. I'll set the timer for two minutes. Start matching pairs of shoes by placing your hand beside the shoe that matches the one someone else is wearing. You may have to lean over someone or crawl under a player to match the shoes. We'll have a jumbled domino board when we're through, but let's see if everyone can find a match before time runs out.**

Play until time runs out or until all the shoes have been matched.

INSIDE TIP

This is a good ice-breaker game for the beginning of the year. Have kids exchange shoes and names when they're done playing.

iNDEXES

ALPHABETICAL iNDEX oF GAMES

GAMES BEST FOR:

EARLY ELEMENTARY (K-3)

UPPER ELEMENTARY (GRADES 4-6)

ALL AGES (K-6)

LOW-ENERGY GAMES

MEDIUM-ENERGY GAMES

HiGH-ENERGY GAMES